GEMS
Of Encouragement

*Since my youth, God, you have taught me,
and to this day I declare your marvelous deeds.
Even when I am old and grey, do not forsake me,
my God, till I declare your power to the next generation,
your mighty acts to all who are to come.
Psalm 71:17-18 NIV*

By
SYBIL BRODIE

Copyright © 2014 by Sybil Brodie

Gems of Encouragement
by Sybil Brodie

Printed in the United States of America

ISBN 9781498413046

All rights reserved solely by the author. The author guarantees all contents are original and do not infringe upon the legal rights of any other person or work. No part of this book may be reproduced in any form without the permission of the author. The views expressed in this book are not necessarily those of the publisher.

Scripture quotations taken from the Holy Bible, New International Version (NIV). Copyright © 1973, 1978, 1984, 2011 by Biblica, Inc.™. Used by permission. All rights reserved.

The New King James Version (NKJV). Copyright © 1982 by Thomas Nelson, Inc. Used by permission. All rights reserved.

www.xulonpress.com

TABLE OF CONTENTS

Introduction ix
Dedication xiii
Acknowledgments xv

PART ONE – BEGINNINGS 19

   Soldier's Harvest 21
   Fit For His Service 26
   Meeting My Maker 30
   Do Not Fear 33
   Long Long Ago 37
   Marriage – 'Till Death Do Us Part 43
   Guard Change 49
   Lukewarm Christian 53
   The King 57
   Plankety Plank Plank! 60
   Resurrection Day 65
   My Life is but a Weaving 69
   Does Worship Matter? 70
   My Moment As A Scrutinizer 73
   Light Of The World 77
   O GRACIOUS LIGHT 81
   Mission Impossible 82

PART TWO – LESSONS LEARNED........ 87

Why Me Lord?......................... 89
Fresh Encounters 91
Prayer................................ 95
The New Jerusalem 101
A Merciful Attitude Of Forgiveness 105
Amazing Love! 108
Dijon Vu – Same Old Mustard As Before!.. 112
Hands Open Or Closed? 116
Different Gifts 120
Fellowship 123
A Sure Way To A Happy Day 126
Lover Of My Soul 127
Wisdom 128
Rowdies In Our Midst 134
Change In An Ever Changing World 139
Strength Of Faith 144
Discouragement...................... 152
Your Attitude 156
My Way Or God's Way 160
No Shots Fired....................... 167
If Jesus Came To Your Church 172
Let Me Trust In You Lord 176
The Bible Banned, Burned, Beloved...... 177
Which File Or Pile................... 183

Table of Contents

PART THREE – HOMEWARD BOUND 189

Let The Son Shine In 191
Honestly Honest 194
Fishers Of Men 198
Disciple Or Apostle 202
Name Calling 205
What Love 209
Old Broom – New Broom 211
Old Body Young Eyes 215
Just Enough 219
1912 – A Very Good Year 222
Death'S Vice 228
When Heaven Is My Home 231
Lifeblood 232
The Fig Tree 235
A Shepherd'S Love 237
I Had A Dream 243
A Brighter New Year 250
The Difficult Job Of A Guardian Angel 255
Lantern & Anchor 258
Disappointment – His Appointment 261
Anxious Prayers 264
Faith Like Solomon Or Jabez 265
Further Encouragement 269

INTRODUCTION

When I was a young girl of eleven, we moved from Red Lake, a northern mining town in Ontario, Canada, south to the town of Bracebridge. I say south because in Red Lake we would sometimes have a snowstorm in June.

    I attended a rural school on the edge of town where I met Ann Taylor who would become my best friend. It was at this time that Ann invited me to attend the Salvation Army. Since I lived out of town, I had to spend the weekend in town at her home. While attending church with her, I was introduced to Jesus in a way this Catholic girl had never known. I became a 'born again' Christian, or as it was known then, 'saved.' I spent a lot of weekends at Ann's as well as a lot of time on street corners singing hymns accompanied with a drum and horn.

    I married when I was seventeen, and my husband, Neil, was twenty-five. We were blessed with *four children — Tim, Karen, Robert and Garth, who are all serving the Lord in various ways.*

When I look back over the years I find most of my adult married life was spent doing things my way rather than God's way. My ignoring spiritual warnings while embracing worldly pursuits not only brought me much grief, but grief to others around me.

In my early fifties God said to me... "Enough!" He never gave up on me while mercifully bringing me back into His fold. This is something this Saint has never fully understood. I often wish I had heeded His callings years earlier to escape those many dry decades away from my loving Savior. But then I would not be the person I am today.

God took this broken vessel and re-formed me into someone He can use to reach out to others who are often suffering the same consequences that I brought upon myself. Thanking Him for not giving up on me or leaving me to my own devices has been my most grateful of prayers.

During my renewal years, Jesus opened doors for me that I was definitely not equipped to handle nor had the necessary skills to fulfill. He made me editor of a yearly newsletter at the church I was attending when I had no training to do this job. Over the years

Introduction

He taught me so many skills while, at the same time, giving me an outlet for my writings. Since that time of change, God has used me in ways that has often left me with my mouth hanging open in amazement.

God opened another door when a Pastor at my next church, allowed me to put together a monthly encouragement, which I named "EncouraGem." I followed that with my own website called by the same name, <u>encouragem.com</u>, along with a Facebook and Twitter pages to promote my website and to reach more people with His messages.

Presently God has me putting these encouraging articles into this book. I pray they will lift you up and inspire you to reach out for Him, the sustainer and giver of life. I encourage you to walk daily with the Lord Jesus so that like me, your life will never be the same.

My mission is to —

"Encourage, enlighten, inspire, teach, to bring joy and laughter, to be positive and upbeat, to love others just as Jesus loves me."

DEDICATION

I dedicate this book to my husband, Neil, who over the years encouraged me to write when I felt very inadequate to do so. He was so good at pointing out the trees when all I could see was the forest. When he found it necessary to gently correct me in regards to my often narrow focus or quick assumptions, I would usually disagree with his assessment before going away to ponder his suggestions. Then, I would come back at a later time when I realized he was right and make the changes that he stipulated. What a blessing he was to help me finally focus on the tree instead of the whole forest.

ACKNOWLEDGMENTS

I would like to thank my children, Tim, Karen, Robert and Garth, along with their spouses, Donna, Jim, Ana and Grace, who have been my biggest fans. Their encouraging comments would always be done in a loving, kindly manner, bolstering my resolve to do better and to keep plugging away.

To my grandson, Matthew, who encouraged me with chats and discussion about his own writings. When his book, "The Shadow Flames of Uluru," Book 1 in the Chaos Down Under series, was published, it gave me the extra boost to pursue writing my own book.

Thanks are due to Doctor Earl Cooper who was Pastor at Pinegrove Baptist Church at the time I was renewing my faith. He was and is to this day an excellent teacher of Scripture. I learned so much from his sermons each week, along with the courses in Theology that he taught at our church. He inspired me to go back to school, at a time when this old gal had not been in a classroom or memorized anything in years. I learned from him about the inerrant truth of the Bible and will be forever grateful for his servanthood to Christ.

I also would like to thank Pastor Don Brubacher who continued to help my maturing in Christ at Riverside Baptist Church through his knowledge of biblical truths. These he imparted in a loving, patient way to everyone. The Fresh Encounters Bible study he faithfully gave each Wednesday was a time where I could bring forward my many questions. They were always answered by examples from Scripture. If it wasn't in the bible, then I was going down the wrong path.

Many thanks belong to my daughter, Karen, who spent many hours proof-reading my manuscript. She brought my attention to errors as well as suggested changes, all of which improved and enhanced the finished product. Her encouragement over the years has always been positive and given with love through her desire that I succeed in the direction of the Lord's leading.

I owe so many thanks to my son, Robert, who lovingly devoted sooo many hours over the years to solving all of my electronic and computer problems.

Acknowledgments

He has downloaded, fixed, corrected, and taught me tirelessly to help me get the desired results. I could not have done any of this without his gifted expertise or without his loving care that I succeed in any endeavor I tackled.

I will be forever grateful to my niece Heather, who freely gave of her expertise in the final editing of my manuscript. What a blessing she was at a very crucial time for my getting it back to my publisher.

My biggest thanks goes to my Savior for giving me the written words to encourage others with His love, understanding, teachings, humor, laughter, and joy to many a hurting or lost soul. He is the one who put together all of these wonderful people at the right place, at the right time, when I needed a helping hand.

To Him belongs all the Glory.

PART ONE-BEGINNINGS

SOLDIER'S HARVEST

"The Lord Is a Warrior–Yes, Jehovah is His name!" **Exodus 15:3**

When I was eleven my girlfriend, Ann Taylor, encouraged me to attend the Salvation Army. This choice may have seemed odd to some for a Catholic girl who had just finished her First Communion, but God was calling me elsewhere.

Ann was born with a severe heart condition and has been with her Savior for many years. In spite of her affliction, she was a good Soldier, and I'm sure she has heard her Savior say, *"Well done my good and faithful servant."*

At that time of my life, the Lord placed on my heart a real yearning to get to know Him better, and I accepted Him as my Savior. Not that I led a very obedient life after that. In fact, this Soldier was

AWOL for most of my earlier years, living my way and not His.

In spite of my disobedience, I eventually learned that I was a recruited soldier in the Lord's Army. As His soldier He wanted to use me to accomplish His purpose. So what was that purpose that God had in mind for me?

Roberts Liardon, in his book *Final Approach*, helps answer this when he says. . . ,

"We are living in the most thrilling exciting time of the church. This generation is privileged to usher in our Lord and Savior, Jesus Christ. Sad to say, however, the way most Christians live is anything but thrilling or exciting. Many Christians seem to have the attitude—Well, I'll just make it the best I can and rejoice when the rapture comes and we all get lifted out of this mess. Christianity is not just a little bless-me club where we all go to get happy... When there are battles to be fought, God always prepares a generation of warriors. The Lord chose us to be His soldiers. This is not a volunteer army; every Christian has been drafted. There are no conscientious

objectors in His army. We are Soldiers, and that's all there is to it!

Of the many Soldiers throughout the Bible that God has used, the one in particular that stands out for me is Jeremiah. God chose him to tell the Israelites about their sin and His truths. But listen to his words, which sound eerily applicable to our present day:

"An astonishing and horrible thing has been committed in the land; The prophets prophesy falsely and the priests rule by their own power; And My people love to have it so, but what will you do in the end?" Jeremiah 5: 30-31

The Israelites did not reward Jeremiah for faithfully obeying God, but instead he was put into stocks while the people mocked and ridiculed him. Distraught, he cried out, *"Then I said, I will not make mention of Him, nor speak anymore His name" Jeremiah 20:9.*

Many of you have been to that point of discouragement; I know I certainly have. But just when I thought I couldn't take any more, God did for me what He did for Jeremiah. He came alongside him, strengthening his heart, mind, and body so that Jeremiah responded with,

"But His word was in my heart like a burning fire shut up in my bones; I was weary of holding it back, And I could not" Jeremiah 20:11.

The Lord of the Harvest is lining up His warriors today just as He has done in ages past. Are you weary like I was of holding back? As His soldier, how will you respond?

Good times; Bad times; End times; Harvest time; **Wasted Time.** We win the race by letting Jesus use us to accomplish His purposes in this end of times battle.

Don't waste your earthly time like I did. Onward Christian Soldier... HARVEST TIME IS HERE.

Onward Christian Soldiers
Sabine Baring-Gould

Onward Christian Soldiers
Marching as to war
With the Cross of Jesus
Going on before
Christ the Royal Master
Leads against the foe
Forward into battle
See His banner go!

At the sign of triumph
Satan's host doth flee
On, then, Christian Soldiers
On to victory
Hell's foundations quiver
At the shouts of praise
Brothers, lift your voices
Loud your anthems raise!

FIT FOR HIS SERVICE

"...always be prepared to give an answer to everyone who asks you to give the reason for the hope that you have." **1 Peter 3:15**

What message will we bring to a non-believing world? Will it be a message of a liberating, light bearing Savior who loves us unconditionally? Or will it be one of an intolerant, legalistic, judgmental God?

For years I have taken to heart the Bible's message to *"Love my neighbor as myself."* Where I fall flat on my face is when Jesus tells me to *"Go and make fishers of men."* That interferes with my comfort zone and perhaps my lazy zone? It is so much easier to sit back and say to myself, *"Let go and let God."* But the real meaning of that phrase is to let go of your way of doing things, and let God do the leading. Let God empower you with His strength to overcome your weakness.

This sounds simple, but in reality how many of us focus on our inadequacies instead of God's strength? How many of us listen to Satan's lies that we are not good enough or smart enough for God to need, let alone use? So we give up or try to do things in our own strength instead of following and listening to our Leader.

I learned years ago that I have a problem with verbally carrying a good theological argument. Whenever I try to tell others about Jesus, I get overly anxious, and what I know in my head does not come out of my mouth. Frustration with myself, along with the other person's frustration with me, quickly ends any meaningful dialogue. At that point, I am usually left begging the question, *"Lord, how can I be salt and light when I turn more people away from you than towards you"?* During these encounters, I never truly feel fit for any service call from God.

Because of my inadequacy in this department, Jesus has mercifully bestowed a much-needed gift upon my discouraged shoulders: the gift of being able to express my love and relationship with Him through my writing. What joy I get from putting words on paper to tell what He has done for me over the years.

God has been answering my ongoing prayer of change regarding this problem by changing both my focus and my attitude: the focus being from my strength to His strength, and my attitude being to get out of my easy chair to begin a different exercise program.

I am learning to choose my spoken words more carefully, and although I don't always manage that well, God continues to urge me forward. He is teaching me to show my love for Him through other means such as my writings, my actions, and my inactions—by loving and caring for those who don't agree with me about Him. I have learned that I don't need to do the Holy Spirit's job; I just need to be able to give an answer to why I believe in Jesus. I think of myself more now as a planter of seeds with someone else doing the watering and harvesting.

If I am to be fit for His service, it is up to me to change by letting go of my fears and trusting in God for the outcome—not an easy thing to do, but a necessary one if change is to occur.

Joseph Stowell's book *"The Trouble With Jesus,"* tells us we can be salt and light by . . .

Declaration–Speaking up for Jesus
Demonstration Showing up for Jesus
Compassion–Reaching out for Jesus
Community–Loving for Jesus
Consecration–Living for Jesus

Today I am ready for my next step forward. I want to align God's goals to be my goals; His desires to be my desires; to care more about relationships than my own achievements. I now want to be more 'Fit For His Service.'

Tell me . . . How fit are you?

"For physical training is of some value, but godliness has value for all things, holding promise for both the present life and the life to come." 1 Timothy 4:8 NIV

MEETING MY MAKER

"I am with you always, even to the end of the age." Matthew 28:20

What is the first thing you think of when you hear the words *Meeting my Maker*? To most people it means they will have died and come face to face with God. I use to see it that way but not anymore. I now realize I met my Maker when I was eleven years old. I went forward when I heard Him calling my name, and there He was!

I was so filled with joy at meeting Him that I went forward again the next Sunday to say, *"Hello, do you remember me?"* I loved the feeling of warmth and love He gave to me.

So much so, that up I went to meet Him again the third Sunday. This time, however, a dear Saint came alongside me and whispered, *"Once is all it takes; you now belong to Jesus forever."*

I do? Questions filled my mind. How can I feel Jesus' love, comfort and acceptance now? Where can I meet with Him if not here? Will He forget me and move on to someone else?

Over the years, the answers to those questions have become very clear. Every time I call upon Him, He will be right there. I will feel His presence, comfort and love immediately, everywhere and anywhere I want to meet with Him.

He will never forget me — It is I who forget Him.

Meeting with my Maker has become a journey into places filled with amazing adventures. For instance, I meet Him every time I pray. I'm drawn to Him when I open my Bible and study His Words, which seem to have been written just for me. It is at these times that I get to know Him more personally.

He speaks directly to me: teaching me, encouraging me, answering my questions, opening my mind to things I would never know or understand without Him. I worship Him most at these times, doors opening the widest. Fresh breezes blowing through my mind until it becomes just my Maker and me ... alone.

Begin your adventure of a lifetime by meeting with your Maker, the one who loves you unconditionally. You will find Him if you seek Him with all your heart. Say *YES* to Jesus and spend eternity with Him in Forever land.

DO NOT FEAR

"God is our refuge and strength, A very present help in times of trouble.
Therefore we will not fear, Even though the earth be removed,
And though the mountains be carried into the midst of the sea;" Psalm 46: 1-2

When I was a young girl of seven or eight, I lived in a little mining town called Red Lake, Ontario, close to the Manitoba border. My father labored in the gold mines to provide for his family, while my mother worked hard tending to the needs of us active children.

I had a distance to go to walk to school and often traversed through a short lane when pressed for time. I hated cutting through that lane because of a little dog that lived in one of the houses and was often out loose. But as children do, I sometimes dawdled along the road and then had to take this dreaded lane in order to not be late for school.

Although this dog was small in size, he was a vicious looking monster to me, and I was very fearful of him. My imagination had him sinking his teeth into my ankle before he jumped up and tore open my throat! I became paralyzed with fear if I saw him, so I would stealthily try to sneak by his house and then run as fast as I could through the lane to the safety of the road on the other end. I was grateful that, for some reason, he never left the lane-way.

One day I had to take this lane back from school because, not being the best-behaved child in class, I had to stay for punishment of one sort or another. It obviously did not achieve the results the teacher was hoping for because I can't remember why I was being punished.

I made the fearful decision to take this dreaded lane back home since I was sure my mother would be worried, or more likely thinking *"What has she been up to now!"*

I was stealthily slipping through the lane when suddenly behind me the monster jumped out of the bushes barking, growling and baring its teeth. I took a quick glance before turning in fearful panic, running as fast as my little legs would take me.

As I ran I could hear and feel him getting closer and closer! Just as I was sure he was getting ready to sink his teeth into my ankle, I turned and in absolute terror screamed at the top of my lungs.

The dog stopped dead in its tracks with a shocked fearful look on its face. It then turned and, with its tail between its legs, ran back home. With my mouth wide open and my body still shaking, I turned and did the same, running for the safety of my home.

I see such a correlation today between that time and what I have learned about fear over the years. First, I would like you to notice that the dog came at me from behind. Second, I now understand why he never left the lane. And third, Satan does the same thing doesn't he? Lurking in the background, coming up from behind, hoping to catch you off-guard while filling you with imagined fears.

The Bible tells us in 1 Peter *"The devil prowls around like a roaring lion looking for someone to devour."* But then it adds, *"Resist him and stand firm in the faith."* In James we are told, *"Therefore submit to God. Resist the devil and he will flee from you."*

Just like this little dog that turned and ran away from me when he was confronted with the fact that I was standing firm – Satan will flee from you when you stand firm in your faith.

When confronted by Satan's roar, stand fast in the Lord. Flee from the devil to the other side of the road, to your home, to the safety of Jesus.

LONG LONG AGO

"Suddenly a sound like the blowing of a violent wind came from heaven and filled the whole house where they were sitting." Acts 2:2

Long, long ago there was a handsome young man who owned a Harley Davidson motorcycle. He loved to jump on his bike and ride fast with the wind blowing through his hair.

He would ride to his job as a principal at a little rural schoolhouse on the edge of town. When he was through there for the day, he rode his Harley to work at the BA Gas Station he owned with his brother-in-law Harry. They both labored hard to make this business and their careers a success.

There was a young lady who lived a short distance out of town that knew the young man because she went to his school. Whenever she came into town she would walk or ride her bike slowly past the gas station, hoping to see the young man. She really liked him, and she felt he liked her too.

When he saw her he would wave, and if he was not busy serving customers, she would stop to talk. She particularly admired his Harley Davidson motorcycle. The thought of riding on it brought her a feeling of excitement mixed with the fear of speeding down the highway on such a powerful machine. That would be so much fun. The thought also entered her mind that in order to keep from falling off she would have to hold on tightly to the young man.

One day when the young man was working at the gas station, the young lady stopped to chat. He tentatively asked her if she would like to go for a ride on his motorcycle. She could hardly believe her ears and was speechless for about two seconds before saying, *"Yes, I would love to!"* So they arranged a day in which to do this. I guess you could call it their first date.

In order to prepare for this special date, the young lady asked her mother if she would perm her hair. She wanted to look her best for this very special event in her life.

The day arrived and out of the house the young lady bounded, feeling so pretty in her newly permed hair. She was filled with excitement for the ride ahead with the handsome young man.

In those days no helmet was required for motorcycles so ladies would sometimes use a kerchief to cover their hair. But this young lady did not want anything to interfere with the experience of this first ride, so she did not bother at all with any hair covering.

She had a little bit of trouble getting her leg over the big bike but managed to do so. The young man asked if she was all set and when she said yes, his next words were, *"Hold on tight!"* So she held her breath and slipped her arms around his waist, wondering at that moment if she had made the right decision.

Off they sped down the highway, and as she closed her eyes in excitement, her breathing seemed to stop while her stomach did flip-flops with the feel of the speed. Finally she dared to open her eyes and then slowly moved her head passed the young mans shoulder. While everything she saw seemed to pass quickly in a blur, the wind blowing over her face and through her hair brought a feeling of exhilarating freedom she had never experienced before.

She felt absolutely no fear because she had her arms tightly clasped around the young man. They rode and rode for miles. She knew there was danger if the young man made a wrong turn or did not see a hole in the road. Still, for some reason she never felt fear with him in the driver's seat, perhaps because she knew he was an honorable young man who cared very much about her well being.

They finally stopped to rest and spent a long period of time talking about everything and anything. When they ran out of time along with words, they got back on the Harley and headed for her home. Upon dropping her safely there, they arranged to meet again another time. Wow! A second date.

The young lady smiled and was in awe of the time she had just spent. She knew right then and there that she loved the young man, and for some strange reason, she knew he loved her too.

As she walked into the kitchen of her home her mother looked up and gasped in dismay... *"What have you done to your hair? Your new permanent is blown straight back into a tangled mess!"* In today's language I guess you could say she had her first—and only—Afro!

The young lady didn't mind as she basked in the glow of the time spent with the young man. She recognized the change was not only in her hair but also in her heart, for she would never be the same person she was before her ride with the young man on his Harley Davidson motorcycle.

This is a true story of love's first bloom between my husband Neil and me as we began our courtship so many years ago. I see a correlation between our young love, and what it is like when you first fall in love with Jesus.

* Right away you just know that He is honorable and trustworthy, with your best interests at heart.
* You know that He cares about your well-being and that he knows where the dangers and potholes lie ahead in your life.
* He will take you out of your comfort zone into adventures that will make you squeal with amazement and delight.
* You may be blown and tossed about by the wind and the speed of this adventure, but if you keep your arms tightly clasped around Him, no harm will come to you. You will emerge at the end so deeply in love with Him.
* As you stop along the wayside and talk with Him about everything and anything, you will get to know Him personally. The time will fly by as you learn all about Him.

* What joy and happiness will envelope you as you begin this journey together.
* I guarantee people will notice the change in your appearance. Not only the glow on your face, but the joy emanating from within you.
* Like me, I guarantee you will never be the same person again.

MARRIAGE – 'TILL DEATH DO US PART

"The Bible talks about marriage as a commitment of a man and woman to wed their lives together lovingly in a union that is total: spiritual, mental and physical." Matthew 19:5-6

One day my granddaughter Lisa said to me...

"Gramma how have you and grandpa stayed together in a relationship with one person for all these years? Didn't you get bored with one another?"

I was surprised by the question at the time and could only mutter something about making a vow to love one another. But that question niggled at the back of my mind, and I've thought since deeply about the why, as well as the how.

Many young people today have no idea about the how and, saddest of all, about the why. Their attitude is, *"Why should I bother?"*

I would love to say that I knew the answers from the beginning of my marriage and that is why we made it well past the fifty-four year mark. However, I made so many mistakes, and there were times over the years when I did feel like running away to start my life all over again with another Prince Charming. So why did I stay, and why did my husband stay with me? I am sure there were times in our marriage when he felt the same difficult stresses and strains as anyone in an intimate relationship.

When I was a child, I loved fairy tales like Cinderella and Snow White. The Prince would come along and fall in love with the scullery maid *(me)* and marry her and make her his Princess. The part I always liked the best was the ending where they *"Lived Happily Ever After."*

Fairy tales and marriage are as far from that reality as Neil was from being a Prince and I was from being a Princess. Besides, as far as I knew princesses didn't make applesauce on their honeymoon, so I knew for sure I didn't have royalty in my background.

The bible tells us in Genesis 2 that God not only created marriage, but also encourages it, and commands unity in it as a lifelong relationship. While it does not condone anyone living in an abusive and dangerous relationship, a marriage vow in Scripture is a binding covenant between a man and a woman to love, honor, and cherish one another for as long as they both shall live.

Perhaps this is the main reason why today's young adults do not understand longevity with one person. Some have never heard or read the Bible, and some don't believe it even if they have read or heard. Many churches today are telling their congregations that some parts of the Bible are myths and some parts are truths. When they do that, they brand the whole book as one not to be trusted. Why would one read or seek out truths from a book that they have been taught are part fairy tales and myths?

I guess therein lies the first reason Neil and I had longevity in our relationship. We were both on the same page with belief: none of the Bible was myth but truth from Genesis to Revelation. Marriage is a hard enough row to hoe without having to compromise, change, or water down one's faith in God.

We believed that the vows we made on our wedding day were to God, and that it was He who brought us together: *"For better or for worse; for richer for poorer; in sickness and in health; until death did us part."* Many couples today would never dream of including the words *'For better or for worse'* in their vows, but we never considered leaving them out.

The second reason takes us back to *"Made applesauce on our honeymoon"* to explain what I learned right from the beginning of my marriage.

The first thing I learned was that life with an enterprising husband would never ever be boring. So that part of my granddaughter's question is easily answered by this old gal's recollection from her honeymoon.

Out for a drive in the countryside, Neil and I came upon this big wild apple tree out in a field, loaded with great big apples. So of course we began to pick and eat some. There were so many of them that before long we had mounds piled in the trunk of the car. Then it dawned on us that we didn't have a pot big enough at our honeymoon cottage to cook them, nor the jars in which to store the cache.

My enterprising husband came up with the obvious solution: take a day trip back to Mom Brodie's house for a free lesson in applesauce making.

So... under her expertise and instruction, we learned that day how to make applesauce. Thus began my many years of preserving different fruits and vegetables that existed in my part of the world. When I look back and remember those times, it is not with disappointment in my honeymoon, but with the satisfaction of a job well done, notwithstanding the fun and adventure we had learning these skills together.

The wonderful food I learned to prepare at such an early time in our marriage brought many blessings to our family and ourselves over the years. Another blessing was getting to know my mother-in-law better by being given a glimpse of how much knowledge she had to share about making a house a home.

I read once, *"Success in marriage is not finding the right person, but becoming the right person."* With my many shortcomings, this 'becoming' has been quite a challenge for me. Seeing the good in someone when one is angry or disappointed with them is a hard adjustment to make. Forgiveness for those disappointments can be harder still but is a must to bring peace and happiness to any relationship. *Pride goeth before a fall* is one Biblical principle that inflicted many bruises on this soul's headstrong opinions.

One thing I learned for certain over the years of our married life was that Jesus is the only third party in a marriage that can make it work. This concept of a third party not only refers to adulteress affairs but also includes preferring to spend an excess amount of time with close friends or family members ahead of your spouse. Doing things together helps you work through problems in a relationship, and it is often the tie that heals and binds many a festering, but hidden, wound.

The Scripture I would pass on to you for a lasting and happy marriage, my dear granddaughter, is 1st Corinthians 13:4-8: *Love suffers long and is kind; love does not envy; love does not parade itself, is not puffed up; does not behave rudely, does not seek its own, is not provoked, thinks no evil; does not rejoice in iniquity, but rejoices in the truth; bears all things, believes all things, hopes all things, endures all things; Love never fails.*

I hope this gives you some answers. I pray for God's grace in the choices you will make. But more than that, may He bless you with a husband, a *'Prince Charming'*, just like your beloved grandfather.

GUARD CHANGE

"But the Lord is faithful, who will establish you and guard you from the evil one."
2 Thessalonians 3:3

I wrote the following poem in August, 1980, while Neil and I were on a camping trip to the East Coast with my mother and father. We had stopped in Ottawa to watch the Changing of the Guard in front of the Parliament Buildings. It was one of the highlights of a trip full of wonderful memories.

November is a time of year that we honor our Veteran Soldiers who have died fighting in wars so that we may live in peace and freedom. We should always remember them and never forget that because of their sacrifice, we live in peace and freedom in a democratic country.

There were also many men who could not go to war but stayed home because of age or medical problems. They looked after their families and did whatever they were able to do to help their country overcome this threat to our freedoms.

My father was one of the men who was unable to enlist because of a hearing problem, but that did not stop him from taking his responsibility to his country and the protection of his family very seriously. He was a perfect example of a loving earthly father that made it so easy for me to see and accept my loving heavenly Father.

My earthly Father died on January 20, 1990, at the age of eighty-four leaving behind a legacy of love to his wife, five daughters and ten grandchildren.

I often thank my heavenly Father for the earthly father He gave to me because my father helped to prepare me for my own Changing of the Guard: the Guard change from my earthly father to my Heavenly Father.

How about you? Have you been able to change your guardianship from your earthly father to your Heavenly Father?

Become one of His Soldiers and Change your Guard today.

THE CHANGING OF THE GUARD

I watched the parade on Parliament Hill
The men in red gave us all such a thrill.
The crowd watched as they left, and they right
Guns all ready with no one to fight.

My Dad and my Mom stood and watched,
eyes aglow
As the band played the tunes they kept time with
their toe,
And the young man beside me whispered
loud the commands
As he became Soldier with gun in his hand.

With tall black fur hats the ritual they followed
Never missing a step as the Sergeant hollered.
They turned heads to left when told, then to right
Then back straight ahead, guns held very tight.

The band took a rest while Inspection was done
As the man in Command looked into each gun.
Then again marched the Soldiers,
bayonets in their hands.
The pageantry gave all a pride in our land.

Once again the band struck up a good beat
The Soldiers all lined up and marched
down the street.
The young man beside me disappeared
in the crowd
As he followed the Soldiers his commands
whispered loud.

I looked to find Mom and Dad to see how
They liked the Parade and Guard Change just now,
I could tell as they smiled from their ear
to their ear
They had a great time and were filled
with good cheer.

LUKEWARM CHRISTIAN

God's love is not some fuzzy thing
That lets us do what we think best;
It guides and warns, and shows the way,
And always puts us to the test. – D. De Haan

In previous years, I had taken part in many Bible studies and courses. A very memorable one for me was with Pastor Earl through Heritage Bible College. I had a great hunger to learn more about the Bible, and true to God's calling Pastor Earl kept the food coming my way. After I finished this course I continued to study the Bible on my own as well as at church. However, by this time in my walk I had drifted into a sporadic spiritual routine with my busy business life taking top priority ahead of my spiritual life.

In reality I had become a ... lazy... lukewarm... armchair... Christian. I was content to sit most of my time in my armchair on the sidelines, and show up on Sundays for my weekly God fix. So by the fall of 2001 my armchair had become a very comfortable one indeed.

Earl Cooper was still the Pastor at this time, and the church had arranged a week-end conference on Henry Blackaby's book, *Experiencing God*, with a study course, '*Knowing and doing the will of God*,'' held in small groups in the following weeks. What the conference began in me, the small group brought together to create an encounter with God that profoundly affected me.

When I first heard the title *Experiencing God*, I thought *"What does that mean? If you've been saved, you've experienced God."* Which is true, but God wanted me to experience so much more of what He had to offer than my armchair ever could.

It was during this weekend conference that He began to change my spiritual life. I will never forget His exact words spoken so clearly to me by the end of the conference ...

"I know your works, that you are neither cold nor hot. I could wish you were cold or hot. So then, because you are lukewarm, and neither cold nor hot, I will vomit you out of my

mouth." Revelation 3:15-16 – Whoa, talk about a revelation!

As if that wasn't hard enough to swallow, He continued,...

"Because you say, I am rich, have become wealthy, and have need of nothing–and do not know that you are wretched, miserable, poor, blind, and naked – I counsel you to buy from Me gold refined in the fire, that you may be rich; and white garments that you may be clothed, that the shame of your nakedness may not be revealed; and anoint your eyes with eye salve, that you may see. As many as I love, I rebuke and chasten. Therefore be zealous and repent." Revelation 3:17-19

At this point with tears falling down my face, I repented. I made a vow to Him right then and there that I would never again be *lukewarm* when it came to worshiping Him.

Since that conference and the courses I have taken that followed, I have experienced God in many wonderful ways.

Every time I go to Fresh Encounters and study the Bible, I experience my Savior. God's Word is always right there in my heart and mind. I see Him every Sunday at church; through the people in the congregation, through godly men and women He has put before me to teach me about Him, through my blossoming prayer life.

God has done things in and through me that I am ill equipped to do, but He continues to use me in spite of my inadequacies and handicaps. I have experiences with Jesus I would never have enjoyed if I had stayed in my comfortable armchair.

But most of all, through coming to know Jesus in such a personal way I can hear His voice, which in turn helps me to make the right choices for my life.

I encourage anyone that is hurting, has hang-ups or habits to turn to Jesus. There is no hurt, hang-up or habit from which He cannot free you.

There is one stipulation, however: like me, you must first get out of your armchair.

"Either we conform our desires to the truth, or we conform the truth to our desires."
Os Guinness

THE KING

Eternal, Immortal, Invisible

"Here is a trustworthy saying that deserves full acceptance; Christ Jesus came into the world to save sinners – of whom I am the worst. But for that very reason I was shown mercy so that in me, the worst of sinners, Christ Jesus might display His immense patience as an example for those who would believe in Him and receive eternal life." 1 Tim. 1:15-16

Have you ever thought of yourself as the *'worst sinner'*, as Paul did in the Scripture above? I know I have. Most of us have a time in our lives that we wish we had listened to that little voice in our head telling us, *"Don't do it!"*, but barreled on straight ahead anyway.

Perhaps that time or times haunt us still as we try to push it from our minds. We go about our lives from day to day with a heaviness on our shoulders, the weight crushing down on our spirits.

We try to slough it off by putting forth a smiling face and forced laughter to pretend our life is just fine.

For a little while we manage to convince ourselves that all is right in our world. But that past action always reappears at a time when we least expect it, along with a gloomy cloud that pours accusations upon us in a torrential downpour.

We are drenched in a blanket of depression. Conviction of our wrong doing brings along a feeling of hopelessness that we will not be strong enough to carry these burdens one more day.

This is absolutely true. We are not strong enough, but read further in verse sixteen:

"But for that very reason I was shown mercy so that in me Christ Jesus might display His immense patience . . .

A glimmer of hope? Yes, but much more than just hope, it is a chance at a full pardon. Paul continues

The King

"as an example for those who would believe in Him and receive eternal life."

Jesus is the One who has patiently waited for you to hand your burdens over to Him. Listen to that inner voice saying *"Do It."* Believe and lighten your load as I did, through a merciful God who longs for you to get to know Him.

There is no pillow so soft as a clear conscience
– ODB

PLANKETY PLANK PLANK!

"Hypocrite! First remove the plank from your own eye, and then you will see clearly to remove the speck from your brother's eye."
Matthew 7:5

Do you notice the Scripture says that it's a *plank* in your eye and just a *speck* in someone else's? For years I always thought that mine was the speck, and everyone else's was the plank. I knew best what other people needed to make their lives happier, even when mine was not a bed of roses. I could say this was my ego exercising itself, and maybe it partly was, but I believe it had more to do with feelings of insecurity. Change can be a threatening experience, especially when it's you God is changing.

After my many flops at telling people what was needed in their lives and the hard lessons I learned,

I do believe I am now seeing my plank more clearly. The more I see it, the clearer my vision becomes towards others, and then what I thought was their plank truly does become a speck.

Take, for instance, last year when I prayed faithfully every day for God to change a certain person that in my view needed drastic change. This is not to say that what I proposed wasn't good or fair; it just was not what was needed in that person's life. However, I believed it was, so I continued to pray and pray for months.

As He always does, God was faithful and answered my prayers in His time. He did as I asked—*but not with whom I asked*. Instead, *He changed me*. He taught me what was truly needed and what was best for that person. I became more understanding of that person's needs; thus my attitude changed.

Once my attitude changed, God changed the circumstances in that person's life. Not in the way I would have done, but in a way that was best for that person.

This taught me more about how God truly loves us. Only He knows our capabilities, strengths and weaknesses. He brought happiness and blessings to that person, which in turn blessed me.

Tell me, is your plank obstructing your view, and getting in the way of blessings for you, as well as others around you? I'm seeing so much clearer now without that plank obstructing my view.

HOPE FOUND

*Sinner
You are saved by grace.
Sinner
since I took your place
Sinner
I have set you free
from your chains of iniquity.*

*Sinner
come to the Cross
Where sinner
I welcome the lost,
and offer you liberty
taking your place
on Calvary's tree.*

*Lost
in earth's gloomy haze
Searching
a way through the maze.
Come,
take Me by the hand
I am JESUS,
the great I AM.*

*I died to set you free
to offer a life with Me.
Freedom
from your life of sin,
My loved one
won't you let Me come in.*

*Sinner
please open the door
to your heart forevermore.
Your sin I will gladly bear
Repent
and these words you'll hear...
Sinner
now saved by My grace.
Sinner
I took your place.
So as Sinner
you'll no longer be known,
But SAINT!
Welcome to God's Throne.*

RESURRECTION DAY

"And Jesus Christ our Lord was shown to be the Son of God when God powerfully raised Him from the dead by means of the Holy Spirit." Romans 1:4

Contrary to popular belief and media mania, Easter did not come about by cute little bunnies, Easter egg hunts, chocolate candies, or fuzzy little lambs. Easter came to us through the sacrifice of a loving God who gave His life for us in order to open the pathway into eternal life. Many Christians refer to Easter as *Resurrection Day*. The day our Lord Jesus Christ rose from the dead.

Over the centuries and to this day, innocent people have suffered punishment and death by false accusers. We are incensed when we hear of these happenings. Yet today we are not incensed when Jesus name is used as a swear word, when He is maligned, ridiculed, or referred to as just a *good man*.

More Christians have been martyred for belief in Jesus in the last hundred years than in all the centuries since His resurrection. Maligning or denying Him is increasing proportionately, as biblical prophecy declared would happen. It is destined to get worse before His second coming.

God, however, continues to turn bad things into good, and this is why Jesus' death on this particular Friday became known as *good*. He could have saved Himself, but He did not because of His love for the very people who tortured and murdered Him—guilty undeserving people just like you and me.

I know of no other professed *god* that has died for mankind, or that has been *resurrected* from the dead. Their graves are not empty but full. Their bodies can be found. But no one has been able to find Jesus' body, and they never will because He has risen.

Jesus very words to Martha were,

"I am the resurrection and the life. He who believes in me will live, even though He dies; and whoever lives and believes in me will never die" John 11:25.

This is the choice that Jesus has given to all mankind and therein lies the rub—the abrasion that incenses people. We want to dictate to God what His terms should be for our lives.

If you think that Jesus is misleading mankind, ask yourself why believers of that day and to this day, chose death and suffering ahead of a continuation of their life when they could easily have saved themselves by just recanting their belief in the resurrection of Jesus?

The answer to this question lies in Romans 1:

"Through Christ, God has given us the privilege and authority to tell Gentiles everywhere what God has done for them, so that they will believe and obey Him, bringing glory to His name."

To faithful believers around the world, Jesus' Resurrection is what Easter is all about. We celebrate the only hope given to mankind by a merciful and loving God.

The Apostle Paul's words from his jail cell in Philippians 3:10-11 says it all:

"I want to know Christ and the power of His resurrection and the fellowship of sharing in His suffering, becoming like Him in His death, and so, somehow, to attain to the resurrection from the dead. Not that I have already obtained all this or have already been made perfect, but I press on to take hold of that for which Christ Jesus took hold of me."

Let Christ Jesus take hold of you just like He took hold of me when I was a young girl of eleven years. Although I spent many years living by my own choices, and suffering the consequences of those choices, once He took hold of me, He never let me go. He won't let go of you either, but of course, first you have to believe in Resurrection Day.

MY LIFE IS BUT A WEAVING
Linda Nichols

My life is but a weaving between my Lord and me,
I cannot choose the colors He works so steadily.
Oft times He weaves in sorrow, and I, in foolish pride
Forget He sees the upper, and I the underside.
The dark threads are as needed in the
Weaver's skillful hand
As the threads of gold and silver in the pattern
He has planned.
Not till the loom is silent, and the shuttles cease to fly
Will God unroll the canvas and explain
the reason why.

DOES WORSHIP MATTER?

"I, John, am the one who heard and saw these things. And when I had heard and seen them, I fell down to worship at the feet of the angel who had been showing them to me. But he said to me, 'Don't do that! I am a fellow servant with you and with your fellow prophets and with all who keep the words of this scroll. Worship God!" Revelation 22:8-9

What is worship, and why does it matter? Contrary to popular belief, it isn't just about church music — the instruments, the songs, the singing, or the singers. It isn't about having a *Rock Star* image, although they are often the focus of our worship. It isn't about the sermon: power point, sound, announcements or communion.

It most certainly is not about *me*! I may desire to be worshipped, but I am unworthy of worship because I have not paid the price.

So what is the real meaning of worship?

Worship is all about who really deserves the glory. Worship is about serving the *ONE* who *has* paid the price. Worship is all about God. His Greatness. His Goodness. His Majesty. His Splendor. His Sacrifice. His Gift of Eternal Life. His Worthiness.

So what, in reality, is my role in worship?

First and foremost, I must be *'born again'* to understand who or how to worship God *(John 3:3)*. I must be a voice He can use, a signpost who points people to Him. I must be a trusted friend of the Bridegroom. I must boast about Him and not about myself. I must be a steadfast faithful servant, inspiring others to seek faith in Him. I must sing His praises for the Bible commands me to sing *(Ephesians 5:16)* and to play instruments *(1Samuel 10:5)* and even to dance with joy *(Ecclesiastes 3:4)*. All for and to Him, for no one else is worthy of my worship.

I must tell the coming generations about Him. My sons, daughters, grandchildren, great grandchildren *(Joel 1:3)*. I must listen carefully to His words and worship wisely. I must put all my hope in Him, the God of the Bible, The Triune God, Father, Son, and Holy Spirit. I must and will exalt and magnify His name and only His name.

Does Worship Matter? Yes, but only if I worship the One who earned the right to be worshiped when He gave up His life as a ransom for my own. That is the only Worship that matters to a Holy God.

MY MOMENT AS A SCRUTINIZER

"A merry heart is like a medicine —
It's soothing for your sadness, gives you joy;
So lift your voice and let your spirit soar —
True happiness is yours without alloy." Hess

I attended a business meeting in which the church members were voting for new Elders, Deacons, Treasurer and Clerk.

Before the meeting began, Jim W., Chair of the meeting, asked me if I would consider being a Scrutineer for the vote. I quickly said, *"Yes, I will be happy to help out."*

He began to walk away when the thought hit me, *"I have never done this before"*, and so I quickly said, *"What does a Scrutineer do?"* He replied *"All you have to do is hand out the ballots, gather them after they are marked, and then count the votes for each position."* *"Oh, I can do that,"* I replied.

I took my seat and the meeting began as Jim W. *(hereafter known as J.W.)* opened the meeting by asking for someone to make a motion to begin. I brushed some hair back from my eye and J.W. says, *"Sybil makes a motion to begin and is there a seconder?"* I said, *"What? Oh, sure,"* raising my hand up farther. Slow is not the name for my body, which is always moving two microns ahead of my brain.

J.W. asks for a seconder and thus the meeting began, along with my first attempt at being a Scrutineer.

Very quickly *(body quickly)* I had to hand out ballots, then realized I hadn't filled out my own yet, so I rushed to my seat, picked up my pen, and accomplished the task. By now it was time to pick them all up again. *"Hooray!"* I thought, *"I've accomplished the first two steps with relative ease. One step to go and my stint as a Scrutineer will be but a memory."*

J.W. leads us Scrutineers, Jim L. *(hereafter known as J.L.)* Justin T. *(hereafter known as J.T.)*, and me, S.B., into the front office and we begin to separate the ballots into piles of 'For and Against.' *"This is a cinch,"* I think. *"We will be out of here in no time!"*

Oh-Oh. Problem number one. *"Hey, fella's,"* I say. *"This ballot has some boxes not ticked off and left blank. What should we do about this?"*

J.L. takes the situation in hand and dutifully goes out to inquire from the powers that be and comes back to tell us what we have to do. Okay, we are on our way once again.

That is, until J.W. comes back to give any aid he can to us novices. We mention the solved problem, to which he replies, *"No, it isn't solved that way, it's solved this way!"* About this time the powers that be that gave J.L. the first solution came in to inform us, *"After some consultation, this is the way it should be done,"* which was the same way as J.W. had just told us to do it. So we were on our way once again with problem number one and two *(even though they were the same problem)* solved.

Satan loves to see us sweat! Knowing that we have a room full of people waiting for the results, he has *problem number three* rear its ugly head. The electric calculator J.W. is trying to use to figure the percentages is not turning on.

I keep mumbling about having a calculator in my purse back in the Sanctuary, but for some reason, I had it in my mind that I couldn't leave the room. Kind of like a sequestered jury. The fact of J.L. having left the room previously never enters my mind!

"Ummmm," I wonder, *"is this like baseball with three strikes and we're out? Will they replace us with three more Scrutineers?"* Well, if so, J.W. is now sidetracked with the calculator problem.

Even though I did well in math at school, I have problems in regards to new math *(nowadays, any math for that matter)*, so I am happy to have J.L. quickly calculate the percentage out of his head that makes perfect sense to me! But then, all of a sudden, J.W. is able to get the calculator working.

Hooray. J.W., J.L., and J.T. immediately begin figuring the percentages, while S.B. makes a comment of a questioning nature. They assure me of the validity of the numbers, and we are able to happily state the winners.

We shred the papers and give the ballots to J.W. Our time as Scrutineers is finally over so J.L., J.T., and S.B. return to their seats.

"Whew! Being a Scrutineer is a hard job, right fellas?" I'm sure poor J.W. would agree. *"Do you think he'll ever ask for our expertise again?"*

For some reason he never did, and with what I learned I'm sure I would be much better at it the second time around.

LIGHT OF THE WORLD

"There shall be no night there; and they need no candle, neither light of the sun; for the Lord God giveth them light; and they shall reign for ever and ever." Revelation 22:5

Light of the World. What does this mean to the average person on the street? The first thing that comes to most minds is the *Sun*; after all, without the sun the world would be in darkness.

Webster's Dictionary defines light as, *"Electromagnetic radiation that can be perceived by the normal unaided human eye; Brightness; The illumination from a source of light; Daylight."*

It defines darkness as *"Having little or no light. Dismal; Gloomy; Obscure; Unenlightened; Ignorant; Dim; Murky."*

From these definitions one can conclude that light brings comfort, sureness, trust, ease of movement and peace of mind, while darkness brings discomfort, unease, tenseness, confusion and danger of the unknown.

Christians believe that the *Son* not the *Sun*, is the light of the world. Jesus is quoted in John 8:12 as saying,

"Then Jesus spoke to them again saying, 'I am the light of the world. He who follows Me shall not walk in darkness, but have the light of life'."

When I was young I happily ran to Jesus' light. This light made me feel loved, comforted, joyful, and I embraced it wholeheartedly. When I grew into my teens and married I slowly drifted away from the light. The cares, burdens and worldly pleasures seemed a better way to solve my problems.

As the years flew on by, I began to turn on other lights because I was told there were many bright lights of this world, not just One, so I continued to search for these new lights. In reality and in my growing darkness, they were dim lights of self-reliance, self-importance, self-indulgence, self-centeredness, self-absorption, selfishness, self...

As I immersed myself in this light, it became so dim that I began groping and searching for a brighter light. I reasoned, *"There must be a switch around here somewhere?"* However, the more I searched, the darker it became until one day I saw no light at all. If these were the lights of the world, who blew them out? I cried out against the darkness that had completely enveloped me. A frightening, grasping panic pursued me wherever I turned, day after day.

Then one day I happened to catch a tiny speck of light. Memories of its warmth flooded my soul, which encouraged me to take one tiny step towards it...

The darkness hissed at me,

"You're not going back there? You'll be rejected! You're not worthy! That speck of light will be extinguished before you can reach it!"

Ignoring what it said, I kept walking towards it even though I knew I was unworthy of any forgiveness. But still I longed for the light I once knew.

"Jesus! Where are you? You loved me once before, forgave me, maybe... maybe you would have mercy on me and do so again?"

Suddenly the darkness was gone, and I was bathed in the brightest light my eyes had seen in years. I felt the same joy. I felt loved, cleansed, enveloped in happiness. But most of all I felt at peace, cradled in the arms of the One and Only true Light of the world.

I once was full of self, and proud
Just like a Pharisee,
Until one day, quite by surprise,
I caught a glimpse of me.
Hawthorne

O GRACIOUS LIGHT
The Book of Common Prayer

O gracious Light,
pure brightness of the ever living Father in heaven,
O Jesus Christ, holy and blessed!
Now as we come to the setting of the sun,
and our eyes behold the vesper light,
we sing your praises, O God:
Father, Son, and Holy Spirit.
You are worthy at all times to be praised
by happy voices,
O Son of God, O Giver of life,
and to be glorified through all the worlds.

MISSION IMPOSSIBLE

"Do not store up for yourselves treasures on earth, where moth and rust destroy, and thieves break in and steal. But store up for yourselves treasures in Heaven." Matthew 6:19-20

The saying goes that negative things happen in threes. That seemed to be the case with electronic machinery at my house recently. First our electric kettle sprung a leak, threatening to electrocute us. Then the answering machine bit the dust, and last but not least, my *"Oh, I'm so used to you"* printer died.

By this time, I felt like I was in an old episode of Mission Impossible, and they had all self-destructed into a puff of smoke.

I had my printer for only five years, and I mentioned this to the company troubleshooter I called for help. After I explained what was happening to the machine he replied, *"Five years is a long time for a printer. You did very well."* How come I didn't feel like I was doing very well?

He also gave me the number for the closest repair station while adding, *"Usually it costs more to have them fixed than to buy a new one."*

I called the repair shop, and he said, *"It's twenty dollars to look at it, and you'll have to get it here somehow* (they were a seventy-five minute ride away). *Then we'll tell you what is wrong and the cost of repairing it."* He added, *"Most people find it is usually cheaper to buy a new one."*

By this time I'm calculating my time, gas, car wear-and-tear, the twenty dollars plus the repair costs, then gas and time back to get it or to pay for shipping. That is when I made the decision I always make at this point with my electronic problems: I called my son Robert! Robert is my *Helppp...er* whenever I am sinking in electronic quicksand.

Robert listened to my explanation of what was wrong with my printer, asked a few pointed questions of me, then said,

> *"Mom, face it: the printer is dead. It will probably cost you more to fix than to buy a new*

one. *You'll get more features with a new one anyway, and pay a lot less than you did for this one.*"

Mission Impossible memories flooded back to my mind:

"*We will disavow this conversation ever took place or that we know you. You have five seconds before this tape self destructs.*"

Poof! There goes my faithful printer in a puff of smoke.

Robert was right, of course. I got a replacement with more features for one third of what I paid for the old one. However, it didn't change the fact that the dead one had been quite adequate for my needs. Nor did it take in all the problems I had getting the new one hooked up.

I am now back to studying the *how to* manual, trying to figure out *how to* use all the extras and *how to* make them work.

Here on earth there is no stopping the need to continually replace things that wear out or break down. I see a correlation between machines and our bodies.

Well, our bodies are often referred to as running like a well-oiled machine.

As my imagination takes wing, let me play out this scenario...

Like these machines, you start out all new and fit in your young body, going happily through the years when suddenly—*Poof*— your body seems to self-destruct.

You call the knowledgeable contact that tells you how lucky you are to have gone on so long with such old equipment, but it doesn't seem old to you.

He repairs you with some grease and oil, patches, new joints, new valves, new pipes, new batteries. Then you begin learning *how to* use all the new equipment to keep you running for a while longer. He says that you can't expect to be like a new model that can do twice the work and have all those up-to-date working features.

When he can't help you any further, he sends you to the next repairman who eventually says, *"Sorry, you need a new body. It will cost way too much to save and repair you."*

New? Repair? Save? I have a Savior! In fact, my Savior does Mission Impossible Miracles!

So I cry out, *"Jesus Helppp...er, Help me."* Poof. *"Wow! Now this is a perfect body. Thank you, Lord."*

PART TWO – LESSONS LEARNED

WHY ME LORD?

Why me, Lord?
Why choose me Lord?
A silly, sometimes brainless person
who is often ungrateful for all you
have done and suffered for me.
Many times I have lusted for things,
but of course, labeled it a 'need.'
I am often argumentative,
as you well know, as I have tried to
persuade You, along with others,
that my way of thinking is the only
way of looking at a problem.
Some could even label me
uncooperative or bull headed and
be right on the mark.
You also know that I am very set in
my ways, that you have to ease me
into accepting changes in my life

in order to work through me.
Oh...but I love it when you work through me, Lord.

*But I don't want to change. I find it
very comfortable in this life you
have given me.
Remember, it is the place You put me,
so You have only Yourself to blame for
my lack of enthusiasm to change.
Right? Right? Answer me Lord.
How come I can't hear You?*

*Why do I get angry with You, Lord?
Why do I lash out at You when I can't
get my way or think You should be
tending to the injustices
that are all around me?
You, the One who loves me more than
I could ever comprehend!
So I often ask myself...
Why choose to save me Lord?
I never would have chosen me...
But... thank you for choosing me.
Your bull-headed, argumentative servant,
Syb.*

FRESH ENCOUNTERS

"Let the peace of Christ rule in your hearts, since as members of one body you were called to peace. And be thankful. Let the word of Christ dwell in you richly as you teach and admonish one another with all wisdom, and as you sing psalms, hymns and spiritual songs with gratitude in your hearts to God."
Colossians 3:15-16

For quite a few years I attended a Wednesday Bible study called Fresh Encounters. If someone were to ask me what the one lesson was that sticks in the forefront of my mind, I would state unequivocally, *"I was shocked to learn we don't work when we get to heaven!"* DON'T WORK? How can that be? What does one do with one's time? Pastor Don pointed out that there is no Scripture to support this thinking of mine. From where then did I get this idea?

I went home and immediately searched the Scriptures. This can't be right! But, no matter how hard I searched, it was nowhere to be found. I thought for sure I was going to help build the New Jerusalem. But the Bible tells me God is going to do that by Himself. For some strange reason, He doesn't need my help.

Over the years I found work helped me cope with disappointments or problems happening in my life. Work is a wonderful outlet that makes me feel needed, loved, useful and fulfilled. What will replace that for me in Heaven? So I began to search the Scriptures to get some understanding, and perhaps a glimpse of what I will be doing in Heaven.

Here is what I found… Heaven is a place prepared for believers where we will spend eternity with God (John 14:1-3). God will be with me and wipe every tear from my eyes, and I will experience no pain or sorrow (Revelation 21:3-4). I won't need a light as God will supply all the light (Rev. 22:5). It will be in Heaven that we will be like Christ and will recognize one another (1 John 3:2). My treasures are to be found in heaven, not on earth (Matthew 6:19-21).

Heaven is only for the righteous who has accepted Jesus as their Savior (Matthew 25:31-46). I was further encouraged to find the Lord Jesus Christ... will transform my lowly body so that it will be like His glorious body (Philippians 3:20-21). I really liked that part because as my pendulum swings forward I think, *"Man do I need a new body."*

I was further encouraged when it told me only those with faith in Jesus will be the inhabitants of Heaven: *"And without faith it is impossible to please God, because anyone who comes to Him must believe that He exists and that He rewards those who earnestly seek him"* (Hebrews 11:6). That means I will have fellowship in Heaven with loved ones who have gone on before me.

The clincher for me was, *"for anyone who enters God's rest also rests from his own work, just as God did from His"* (Hebrews 4:10). I won't need to work to overcome my problems because I won't have any problems.

Lord Jesus, I'm warming up to this plan of yours. You build and work while I rest in You.

REST IN YOU? Hmmm, here's another thought, Lord. Perhaps I could rest in You while here on earth, *before* I get to Heaven. What's that you say? You've been trying to tell me that for years? Do you think perhaps a few more weeks at *Fresh Encounters* might help?

PRAYER

"Then you shall call, and the Lord will answer;
You shall cry, and He will say, 'Here I am.'"
Isaiah 59:1

The prayers of others: how often have they helped me when I was not even aware someone was praying for me? How effective are my own prayers when I pray?

Trusting in prayer as an effective weapon in countering my struggles did not happen to me overnight, but over a period of time. In the past I felt God had much bigger problems to look after besides my pitiful, often self-centered calls for help. Only when I was at the end of my rope would it finally dawn on me that I had left Him completely out of the picture.

As I grew in my faith and continued in my study of the Bible, I became aware of the many answers provided to me about prayer in Scripture.

The most recognizable passage by Christians on how to pray is the Lord's Prayer found in Matthew 6:9-13:

"This, then, is how you should pray: Our Father in heaven, hallowed be your name, your kingdom come, your will be done on earth as it is in heaven. Give us today our daily bread. Forgive us our debts as we also have forgiven our debtors. And lead us not into temptation but deliver us from the evil one."

Matthew 6:6 inform us what we should do when we pray:

"But when you pray, go into your room, close the door and pray to your Father, who is unseen. Then your Father who sees what is done in secret, will reward you."

The Old Testament in Jeremiah 29:12-13 elaborates on that when it says,

"Then you will call upon me and come and pray to me, and I will listen to you. You will seek me and find me when you seek me with all your heart."

Another interesting point about prayer is found in Matthew 6:5 and verses 7-8 which relates how God does *not* want you to pray, which is just as important as how to pray:

"And when you pray, do not be like the hypocrites, for they love to pray standing in the synagogues and on the street corners to be seen by men. I tell you the truth, they have received their reward in full." And *v7-8: "And when you pray do not keep on babbling like pagans, for they think they will be heard because of their many words. Do not be like them, for your Father knows what you need before you ask him."*

As I studied more about prayer, I began to realize it was God's way to develop a closer relationship with me. I learned to rely more on Him through my hardships, while recognizing He also supplies all my joy that carries me through. The more I talked with Him, the more my anxieties decreased and peace seemed to reign in my heart even during chaotic, difficult times.

A few years back I was asked if I was interested in joining our Church Prayer Team. I was at a point where I felt more comfortable about my prayer life, but was still far from where I thought I should be. Still, I accepted the challenge: after all, how hard could it be?

Well, at times I have felt very inadequate to the task. The reality of how many people were in need of prayer was sometimes daunting until I realized what a privilege I had been given.

The more I turned to prayer, the more the answers kept coming to the forefront of my mind. I learned to pray on the spot, or out loud with others listening. This was not an easy thing for me, but the more I did it the more I was given the right words.

We often expect God to answer our prayers immediately as well as in the way we think is best. Fortunately for us, God sees way beyond our scope of time and knowledge. Learning to rely on His answers took faith and a trust that He never makes a mistake. It may be a short period of time for some answers, yet take years for others, but an answer will come—just sometimes not the one I was wanting or expecting to receive.

There have been times in my life that I could not pray because of my own pain, grief or exhaustion. At those times God mercifully placed others around me that prayed for me in my stead. He continued to provide the comfort and peace I needed until I was able to converse with him once again. Only God knows the number of people who have and are at this moment, praying for me, but this brings me great comfort to know He hears and listens and acts on my behalf.

Ruth Bell Graham had this to say about prayer,

"Satan fears prayer because God hears prayer..... Start praying where you are, as you are, about whatever concerns you, about whatever is lying most heavily on your heart, about whatever is irritating or frustrating you at present."

That has helped me a lot when trouble came barreling into my life; I learned to turn to prayer right out of the starting gate. Prayer is no longer my last line of defense but has become my first offensive move for any help I need, no matter how small. I may not receive the answer I was hoping for, but I now know it will be the best answer for my life.

If you find yourself in need of prayer, I urge you to first pray, then call someone you know who will also take your problem to God. Most churches have a prayer chain that will petition the Lord on your behalf. Put your trust in Him to see you up and over any hurdle.

William B. Bradbury wrote the hymn *Sweet Hour of Prayer*. The first verse would be a good one to memorize and goes like this:

Sweet hour of prayer, sweet hour of prayer,
That calls me from a world of care
And bids me at my Father's throne
Make all my wants and wishes known!
In seasons of distress and grief
My soul has often found relief,
And oft escaped the tempter's snare
By thy return, sweet hour of prayer.

THE NEW JERUSALEM

"Revelation 21:1-22"

The book of Revelation has always been a favorite of mine. Not just for the end of times prophecies, but after our time of testing is over, it talks about the new heaven, the new earth, and the new Jerusalem in this way:

"Then I saw a new heaven and a new earth, for the first heaven and the first earth had passed away, and there was no longer any sea. I saw the Holy City, the new Jerusalem, coming down out of heaven from God, prepared as a bride beautifully dressed for her husband. And I heard a loud voice from the throne saying, 'Look! God's dwelling place is now among the people, and he will dwell with

them. They will be his people, and God himself will be with them and be their God.'"

The description it gives of the New Jerusalem I find intrigues me:

"It shone with the glory of God, and its brilliance was like that of a very precious jewel, like a jasper, clear as crystal. It had a great, high wall with twelve gates, and with twelve angels at the gates. . . The wall of the city had twelve foundations, and on them were the names of the twelve apostles of the Lamb. The wall was made of jasper, and the city of pure gold, as pure as glass. The foundations of the city walls were decorated with every kind of precious stone. ... Jasper, then sapphire, agate, emerald, onyx, ruby, chrysolite, beryl, topaz, turquoise, jacinth, and the twelfth foundation was amethyst. The twelve gates were twelve pearls, each gate made of a single pearl. The great street of the city was of gold, as pure as transparent glass" Revelation 21:11-21.

The New Jerusalem

Now my husband and I have done a lot of building over the years, and I cannot imagine the size of this city, let alone using the building materials mentioned here.

Revelation informs us there will be no temple (churches) because the Lord God and the Lamb is its temple. We won't need a sun or moon for God's glory will be its light. There will no longer be any sea because there will be *"the River of the water of life,"* while on each side of this river will be everything we need for food: *"the Tree of Life, bearing twelve crops of fruit, yielding its fruit every month. And the leaves of the tree are for the healing of the nations."*

Nothing impure will ever be allowed to enter this city, only the names of those written in the Lamb's book of life, but *"The cowardly, the unbelieving, the vile, the murderers, the sexually immoral, those who practice magic arts, the idolaters and all liars — they will be consigned to the fiery lake of burning sulphur" (Revelation 21-8, 22-15).*

When looking at Jerusalem today one could fall into a state of depression and hopelessness at what is taking place and happening to God's chosen people, but *John 16:33* encourages us with these words, *"In this world you will have trouble. But take heart! I have overcome the world."*

We have a Savior who gave His life for us so that we would have the choice of choosing Him or Satan, the god of this world. This very choice gives all of us the opportunity of being a part of God's New Heaven, New Earth, and New Jerusalem.

I've made my choice; what about you?

A MERCIFUL ATTITUDE OF FORGIVENESS

"But go and learn what this means: I desire mercy and not sacrifice." Matthew 9:13

When reading this Scripture, three words caught my attention. They were mercy, attitude, and forgiveness, and I wondered about their meaning and how I should apply these words to my life.

So I went to the dictionary and found that mercy meant – *Kind and compassionate treatment; clemency; a benevolent and forgiving pardon when it isn't deserved.* The Old as well as New Testament especially links mercy to God's grace.

Next came attitude, *a position of the body or manner of carrying oneself like your posture. It's a state of feeling or mind about a person or situation.*

In Philippians 2 we get a full understanding of what a person's attitude should be:

"Your attitude should be the same as that of Christ Jesus: Who, being in very nature God, did not consider equality with God something to be grasped, but made himself nothing, taking the very nature of a servant, being made in human likeness. And being found in appearance as a man, he humbled himself and became obedient to death, even death on a cross!"

Last but not least was forgiveness: *to pardon or absolve. To stop being angry about and to excuse a wrong. To forgive is to trust others as if the wrong is forgotten. It includes a new start in attitudes and actions.*

Forgiving others opens us to receive forgiveness from God. Jesus forgives our sins and encourages us to forgive each other the same way.

In spite of the many years that I wronged Him, Jesus' *attitude* towards me has always been one of overwhelming leniency and mercy. His love has left me with an undying gratitude for His pardoning of this undeserving Saint.

We are to treat others just as Jesus has been *merciful* in His treatment of us. In His mercy towards me, He withheld His anger at my wrongdoings and replaced it with compassion, sympathy and forgiveness.

If we do not have this same *merciful attitude of forgiveness*, we will miss out on a myriad of blessings not only to us, but also to others we meet along the way that we know and love.

AMAZING LOVE!

"For God so loved the world that He gave His one and only Son, that whoever believes in Him shall not perish but have eternal life." John 3:16

David prophesied Crucifixion one thousand years before it came into being and it was used in the time of Jesus as a barbaric form of Roman punishment. This horrible way to die was usually reserved for men who were not Roman citizens but guilty of crimes against the Roman government.

When looking at crucifixion — the terrible punishment it inflicted on the body — try to imagine yourself hanging on a wooden cross with nails hammered through the bones of your hands and feet, while you are trying to push upwards through this agonizing pain to let air into your lungs. One can only imagine the horror of dying in such a slow and painful way. Sometimes the soldiers would break your legs so you could no longer push upwards, and at that point death would come quickly.

Evil men have always been capable of such atrocities since the first killing when Cain murdered his own brother, Abel. Why did he do this? Because of jealousy. God recognized his brother Abel's sacrifice as the better one.

Cain was guilty of this first murder, but the sad part is he never felt remorse. He did not see or recognize his wrong doing, just as many of us today do not see our own sin or the need to repent of it.

Now, what if you were innocent of a crime just as Jesus was but falsely accused by others? Would you not come to your own defense and show in whatever manner you could that you were innocent? It is this part of Jesus being accused and refusing to defend Himself that stymies people. They say, *"If He was the Son of God as He claims, why didn't He save Himself?"*

So why didn't He bring forward the proof of His innocence? It was not like He didn't have the opportunity in which to do so. All He needed to do was call down twelve legions of angels to intervene and save Him. But He never did. Why?

We learn why in Isaiah 55:8 where we are told that our way of looking at a problem is not the way God looks at the same problem: *"For my thoughts are not your thoughts, neither are your ways my ways, declares the Lord."*

The sacrifice of goats and lambs was required in the Old Testament to atone for the people's sins. This had to be repeated over and over again for, as we all know, people don't stop sinning. The blood of animals had to be shed each year to keep atoning for all of these sins.

When Jesus gave His life for us on that cross, He became the last sacrifice required. God willingly gave us the perfect sacrifice, His only Son. If we believe in Him, then He will forgive us and save us from our sins. No other sacrifice is needed. The shedding of His blood paid the penalty for our past, present and future sins.

What would that take for anyone to do? It would take an Amazing Love, not mankind's kind of love that requires reciprocation or recognition, but a love so divine, so unlimited in its scope that we cannot begin to fathom or understand it. Would you give your life for those who constantly reject and spew hatred at you? Whereas Jesus' answer to us was words He spoke while hanging on that very Cross, *"Forgive them Father for they know not what they do."*

A quote from Billy Graham gives a glimpse of this kind of love,

"True love is an act of the will—a conscious decision to do what is best for the other person instead of ourselves."

Fortunately for mankind, Jesus' death was not the end of the story but the beginning because three days later He rose from the dead.

His love for us gives us the opportunity to turn to Him in absolute thankfulness for this final sacrifice He made on our behalf that has paid all our debts in full.

Amazing Love: how can it be that thou, my God, wouldst die for me?

DIJON VU-SAME OLD MUSTARD AS BEFORE!

"Then He (Jesus) took a little child and set him in the midst of them. And when He had taken him in His arms, He said to them, Whoever receives one of these little children in My name receives Me; and whoever receives Me, receives not Me but Him who sent Me."
Mark 9:36-37

I was in Los Angeles in February, 2004, looking after my grandchildren who at the time were Sara, seventeen; Amanda, twelve; and Kyle, nine. I was really enjoying the time spent with them and the opportunity that God had afforded me to get away from the cold of Canada to partake in some warmer spring-like weather.

My youngest son Garth is an *idea man*, and his brain is always working out in left field somewhere. He occasionally comes back to earth to gather up the players in order to put his ideas together.

Garth has always had a wonderful sense of humor, and when he was a child he often had me in hysterics. I was told by others that I should have disciplined him with a good kick in the pants; however, I knew God was getting as much enjoyment out of Garth as I was: after all, He made him that way.

However, this story is not about Garth but about his son, Kyle, whom I would describe as a chip off the old block. He has inherited his father's gift of ideas and his wonderful sense of humor.

As I was driving Sara to choir practice, Kyle was chatting in the back seat. What happened next left Sara and I holding our stomachs while I tried to steer the car with tears streaming down our faces from gales of laughter. Here I was in California experiencing a whimsical loving look back at yesteryear. *Dijon Vu–same old mustard as before.*

Kyle began by telling us that his father had informed him they could all get summer jobs when he got his Green Card. He said by then Sara would be nineteen, Amanda twelve, and he would be the ripe old age of eleven.

He continued to elaborate that, for his part, he thought he could get a summer job working with computers. I mentioned that Uncle Tim had Jason and Joshua doing some tasks for him on the computer, so maybe he could do some for his dad.

Kyle immediately dismissed this small thinking of mine and extrapolated that he was thinking of being a computer programmer. He would create programs for customers and charge them the fantastic sum of twenty-five cents a program.

"*Or even better yet,*" he went on, "*I could be a computer salesman as I could make a lot more money selling computers.*" About this time, Sara and I started to laugh, and I blurted out "*Nothing like starting at the top, Kyle.*"

Well, he never let my negative sarcasm deter him in the least, and when he saw he had us on a roll, he began to reel us in.

We passed a Honda Motorcycle dealership, and without missing a beat he said, "*I could be a Honda Test driver. The owner would say to the customer: 'Here's your man; he's going to take you for a test ride.' Then I would say to the customer, 'Don't worry about my height; I was born short.' Or maybe I could be a Taxi driver, and I would say to the customer, 'Come with me and take a ride on death row.' I would stand behind the counter to get the money and the customer would wonder where I was and I would say, 'Hey, I'm down here.'"*

I joined in the fun and said *"Kyle, your dad could stand beside you* (Garth is 6'4") *and say, 'Hi, I'm up here, but don't worry; my son's the man for the job."*

Through blurred vision and sore midriff I managed to get the car to the church and drop Sara off for her choir practice. On the return trip home, Kyle said to me, *"What job did you like best Gramma, and which one do you think I should do?"*

"My dear grandson," I replied. *"You could do all of them with ease, but I really think you should consider another job—that of Comedian."*

> *Happy moments, praise God.*
> *Difficult moments, seek God.*
> *Painful moments trust God.*
> *Every moment, thank God.*

HANDS OPEN OR CLOSED?

"All your children shall be taught by the LORD, and great shall be the peace of your children." Isaiah 54:13

Have you ever taken part in a Vacation Bible Camp week? I have many times, and what a joyful week it can be. So many people offer their helping hands to look after the many children. The responsibility is great for their safety, and yet the volunteers willingly teach, prepare and bring snacks, organize and take part in the games, and work months ahead to prepare the crafts needed, along with the painting of the scenery for the theme being used. It shows the amount of willing hands that are required each year to bring about a successful and happy time for the children.

Nancy Ortberg's book, *Looking for God*, dedicates a chapter to hands. She states,

"Hands! Open or closed, what kind of hands do you have? When it comes to our hands we have a choice. We can either go through life with them closed: tightfisted, fearful, angry, reluctant, withholding, comparative, and empty. Or, we can go through life with our hands open: generous, expressive, grateful, helping, and full."

This brought to my mind one particular year when it was time for the Sunday service following a very active VBC week with many children attending. The church was packed with excited children as well as adults.

It was a very different service than the usual VBC ones of the past; it included a Baby dedication, Teen missions report, update from the Building Committee, as well as a report from our Associate Pastor on Upwards Soccer.

A visiting mother and her small daughter sat next to me in the pew. The little girl was obviously anxious for the program to begin. When it did, she sang and clapped to the songs with great gusto and glee. When it came time for VBC to do their songs and skits, the little girl happily ran to the front to join in with the other children.

Pastor Don gave a short, but very effective message about the *"easy wide road to Hell"* or the *"hard narrow path to Heaven."* He used some of the children from VBC to hold his signs, and then had a small boy go through the narrow door. Talk about *'sign language.'* A person could be absolutely ignorant about the Bible and yet fully understand this simple message by the end of his short sermon to these children.

Just before the last song, the young mother said to me, *"Is your church always like this?"* I was surprised and blubbered, *"Oh no, we usually have two services but because of VBC we're only having one today."* Duh!

She responded, *"No, I mean is your church always so interested in families and children?"*

Oh yes," I replied. *"We're very family oriented."*

I chatted with her after the service, and she said she went to St. Mary's Catholic Church two Sundays a month and tried other churches the other two Sundays. So I mentioned that maybe she would like to come to Riverside for one of those Sundays. She laughed and said she would like to give us a try.

It wasn't until I was lying in bed that night when the light bulb went on in my head—fluorescent light that is, because with me it begins to flicker and then slowly gets brighter.

"Christ's Love." The first time my husband Neil and I came to Riverside we walked into the Sanctuary and were struck by the love that permeated out from the congregation. It seemed to enfold us like a healing balm. It was a feeling of truly belonging to the family of God. It was as if we personally knew the strangers sitting next to us.

This young mother was feeling this same thing when she asked me, *"Is your church always like this?"* I should have shouted from the rooftops *"Yes, Yes it is! Isn't it wonderful?"*

Christ's Church—His Body—can work miracles when Saints reach out to others with loving and willing open hands!

DIFFERENT GIFTS

"We have different gifts, according to the grace given us." Romans 12:6

Romans talks about gifts God has given each one of us but that our individual gifts can't singly do the work that Christ requires of His Saints. Thankfully, people whose gifts and strengths are completely different from ours help to balance our weaknesses, and their abilities make up for our deficiencies. Only by using our gifts together can we be truly useful to Christ.

All congregations have different gifts bestowed on them from God. Gifts like Teachers; Musicians; Singers; Nursery, Youth and Teen workers; Painters; Cooks; Bakers; Administrators; Carpenters; Financial Planners; Electronic Geniuses; and to add to that list, Filing Queens.

What's that you say— *FILING QUEENS?* That's right. It's hard to believe, but someone in our church calls herself the *'Filing Queen,'* and here is how I know.

One of my ongoing complaints of my home office is my many Files and Piles, so you will understand my reaction to this absolutely amazing person of whom I stand in awe.

I used to have my name attached to the Library portfolio, but up to that point, because of my husband's health problems, I wasn't able to lift one finger to help out.

While God was keeping me busy elsewhere, He had His filing queen quietly working in the background, organizing and filing all the books in their proper order! As well, He had her getting ready for the new library that would be going in downstairs. She was cataloguing the books and readying them for the proper space, which had been provided.

About this time God opened my door to being available and nudged me to say something to her about my wanting to help when she was ready. I blurted out *"I am a quick learner, and will do as you tell me, but I am terrible at filing."* To which she quickly replied, *"Oh don't worry about that. I'm the Filing Queen. I LOVE TO FILE!"*

I stared dumbfounded at her for a few seconds while the old song,*"Common-na my house to my house common,"* was dancing around in my head.

I have never heard anyone say they loved filing, let alone that they were the filing queen. But I should have had more faith. God had been grooming someone to take over our library, someone who is His well organized, discerning servant to whom He has given the gift of loving to file. I don't mean to embarrass her by mentioning her name, so I will just say that her mother has a lot of Faythe in Patty's abilities. Obviously, so does the Lord Jesus. What a Savior.

FELLOWSHIP

"Truly our fellowship is with the Father and with His Son Jesus Christ." 1 John 1:3

One of the things I love about Church is the fellowship I share with others who love the Lord. Taking part in all the activities and happenings brings great joy and happiness to my life.

A few years back when my husband's health began to seriously fail, I was not able to partake of this fellowship often, and I missed the fun, laughter and sharing.

For instance, I missed gathering every Wednesday afternoon for bible study at Fresh Encounters. This meeting included singing and bible study, ending with group prayer. It gave a wonderful boost to my spirits during a busy week. Also, I was not able to lend a helping hand at events like the Nurses' Week celebration supper that our church put on for the nurses of our community. Nor could I take part each August in VBC *(Vacation Bible Camp)*, an activity that has always brought me joy, or even just a simple thing like helping our librarian in our very active library. These are just a few of the sharing times with others. Yes, I missed these fellowship times.

But you know what? God knows my needs, and He did not forget me! He sent opportunities my way every day. My love of learning He fulfilled when Dr. Earl Cooper did a four-part series for our church on Serving God in a Wanting World. I spent two enjoyable weeks in the evening hours working through each section of lessons.

Computers can be a bane or a blessing. I find them mostly a blessing! During this time I found so many good Christian sites with authors who inspire and encourage on many subjects that keep the mind active and focused.

I took my Scriptural memory cards with me when I went walking to keep these verses readily available in my mind, or I listened to inspiring songs and music on my iPhone.

My time spent with family, friends and relatives who call, email, or come for a visit was precious and enjoyable hours of fellowshipping for both Neil and me.

My husband and I have always been best friends, so sitting on the back deck enjoying the sunshine or just traveling to see doctors were great fellowship times. Sometimes words were not spoken or needed.

So you see, any trials you are going through can become special times of fellowship. But most importantly for me was the fellowship time I spent with Jesus.

Phil Callaway in his book 'Making Life Rich Without Any Money' says this,

"In a world characterized by loneliness and despair, we can reach out in love to those around us. Or as St. Francis of Assisi once said, 'Preach the gospel all the time. If necessary, use words.'"

Helen Steiner Rice wrote this poem in her book, *Joy for the Heart*. It really says it all.

A SURE WAY TO A HAPPY DAY
Helen Steiner Rice

Happiness is something we create in our mind,
It's not something we search for and so
seldom find,
It's just waking up and beginning the day
by counting our blessings and kneeling to pray,
It's giving up thoughts that breed discontent
And accepting what comes as a gift heaven-sent,
It's giving up wishing for things we have not
And making the best of whatever we've got,
It's knowing that life is determined for us,
And pursuing our tasks without fret, fume, or fuss,
For it's by completing what God gives us to do
That we find real contentment and happiness, too.

LOVER OF MY SOUL

Jesus
Lover of my soul
You paid the price
To make me whole.

You died for me at Calvary
My sins with you upon that tree
Because of You
I am set free.

I've been washed clean
by Your crimson stain
Enabling me to
come home again.

When my time on earth has come,
All my days of toiling done
Looking into the clear blue sky
I'll see all my days gone by.

Walking through heaven's door
These earthly pains I'll feel no more,
And when my body has decayed
You will raise it up whole again.

Jesus
Lover of my soul,
You paid the price
To make me whole.

WISDOM

"If you seek (wisdom) as silver, and search for her as for hidden treasures; then you will understand the fear of the Lord, and find the knowledge of God." Proverbs 2: 4-5

Wisdom. Something we all want to possess, yet it seems to elude the majority of us. At times I think it has completely passed me by. Solomon being blessed with so much wisdom, I thought a prayer asking for just a fraction of what he was given would be of help to me. I'm just sorry I didn't ask for a larger percentage at the time.

"In the multitude of counselors there is safety," so Proverbs 11:14 states. That is one reason I try to seek out wise counselors to multiply my chances of making wise decisions.

I read the true story about Brother Andrew who was a Dutch Missionary. For years he wisely smuggled Bibles into communist countries under threat of death, without once getting caught. His ingenuity under very dangerous circumstances was amazing. He listened to the Holy Spirit, as He guided him safely through some very crucial times of danger.

I was thinking about Brother Andrew one day while looking at a list of questions that Pastor Don gave out one Sunday. The list, written by Don Whitney, of ten questions to ask yourself for the New Year stated, *"Thinking through these questions will help make your year truly life-changing for all of us."* The instructions said to take a 3x5 card and write down ten things you were grateful for in your difficulties. For example, I am grateful that I have a job; I am grateful that I have the privilege to serve the Lord in at least a small fashion; I am grateful that my spouse didn't walk away from our marriage; I am grateful that my son is not on drugs, et cetera. Then put this card somewhere visible. Thank God twice daily for each of these ten things as you begin your day, and before you go to bed:

"Say out loud: 'Lord, I thank you for—.' Every time you think of something critical, replace it with a thanksgiving item from the list. Make sure that you don't mention any of the negative things with which you are struggling. Our mind automatically dwells on negative things, blows small problems out of proportion, and finds something critical in even the good that is happening. That's why we need to have our list ready, so we can immediately replace each discouraging thought with a thankful one. Continue this for twenty-one days until it becomes a habit. You will find incredible changes will take place in your heart and your life as a result."

"OK," I thought, *"That's a good thing!"* After the previous year's roller coaster ride in regards to Neil's health, the word *'life-changing'* catches my eye. I don't know if I can cope with many more life changes at this point. However, God has told me that He will not give me more than I can handle, so I figure I'd better grab a little of Brother Andrew's faith and read on. So I read through the ten questions, trying to

think of an answer. However, I immediately develop a problem. A serious problem.

All of the questions say, *"Think of ONE thing you could do... could ask... most important... single biggest... most helpful... one way... single thing..."* You get the drift? I can't think in singles. When I try to, lo and behold, another thought, idea, person, pops into my head.

Take for example question seven, *"For whose salvation will you pray most fervently this year?"* I think about that and up pops the name of someone I have been praying for, only to be followed by someone else I've been praying for, and soon the list of people I feel need prayer begs to be *the one* whom I should pray for most fervently. I feel guilty if I leave someone out. Single isn't in my brain, only multiples.

So, what to do? I do what I usually do; I seek out wise counsel and trot off to show the list to my husband, Neil. I engage him in conversation to (multiples again) pick his brain for ideas. Strategies, simple solutions, his answers—better yet, his ONE answer.

He states, *"Oh yes, I've read them and take the first one."* I read it out loud, *"What is one thing you could do this year to increase your enjoyment of God?"* *"I've got my answer to that,"* he states. *"You have?" I say."What is it?" But instead of telling me what his answer is, he questions, *"Why? Don't you have an answer?"*

"Yes, I have an answer!" I spit out. *"I have five answers. What I need is to pare it down to one."*

He then goes on to discuss how over the years he has trained his mind to simplify things so that the answer becomes obvious to him and just pops to the front of his mind.

"Hmmmm," I say. "I wish I could say that because I think so deeply on things I have trouble simplifying my thoughts in that way, but we both know that would be hog-wash. We also know there are many times over the fifty-three and a half years of our marriage, that we sometimes have trouble deciphering what each other is actually saying."

"Like right now" I think to myself. *"Why don't you just tell me your answer so my brain can quit hurting?"*

After ten more minutes of 'discussion', I finally state, *"Why don't we do what Pastor Don suggested* and do one question every day? That way we will have time to think about our answers."

"That's a good idea," he says. To which I reply, "I'll make you a copy of the list and put it on your desk."

So far this list hasn't *'life-changed'* anything around here, but it's only January, and the year is still young. Unfortunately, we aren't.

ROWDIES IN OUR MIDST

"For I know the plans I have for you, declares the Lord, plans to prosper you and not to harm you, plans to give you a hope and a future." Jeremiah:29:11

During one annual church meeting I happened to be sitting with a few of what some might call rowdies from a previous church. Now just in case your wondering: *No, they didn't kick us out. We left for reasons of our own.*

During discussion about our present church report, a complimentary remark was made about my work on my EncouraGem articles, and the group attending the meeting applauded. I was feeling awkward about this when one of the rowdies sitting beside me turned and said, *"Looks like your famous. May I have your autograph?"* To this I replied, *"You're bad, Dave,"* and turned and looked at his better half. She, in turn, covered her mouth to stifle a laugh, which of course started me laughing.

Right then someone referred to an error in the report of an incorrect spelling of a person's name. I said out loud to Dave, *"Well, there goes my fame and fortune!"*

About this time I received a disgusted look from a young man across the aisle in the middle section. The look said, *"Please behave yourself and be quiet."*

I felt bad for my outburst, but what can I say: I'm old and haven't been let out much lately!

My human side wanted to add,*"For goodness sake. Lighten up, fellow! This is a meeting, not a funeral."* But I held my tongue because, in spite of of his reaction to my disruption, I know God had him in the 'learning to have patience at any age or situation' time-line.

In spite of the occasional outbursts from us rowdies, I invite everybody I meet to go to church and judge for themselves. If you have never heard the great stories from the Bible, I guarantee you will be in for a wonderful adventure.

Many people attend a church service at Easter, Thanksgiving or Christmas because of loneliness or tradition. Those are great times to do so, but there is so much more to church than a few special services. If you want to see and experience God at work, I guarantee that making friends and enjoying year-round fellowship with others will replace any loneliness that you may be experiencing. Most people are willing to overlook momentary lapses in timing and judgment like they do for me.

If you like to sing, there are plenty of opportunities to join in singing the old as well as the new hymns and songs of worship. Maybe you're a musician? Let me tell you, musicians are always welcome at every church, and your heart will be lifted up as theirs are in praise to God.

Finding a Bible-believing Church is not always easy in this world of *"all religions lead to the same god"* misinformation. Perhaps you will have to attend a few church services before you find one that preaches Jesus as the One and Only way to heaven. I encourage you to begin your search with the Bible, the best His-Story book you will ever read. There you will find the only Savior, Jesus, that was willing to die for you so you could spend eternity in heaven not hell.

A praying church is another guidepost that will help you because they have learned to turn to prayer first, to help them through the same difficult trials you are experiencing. Jesus is the only one who will take and carry your load when you turn in prayer to the Load Bearer. He has carried me through anxious, scary, tumultuous times, and yet filled me with peace that certainly did surpass all my understanding.

The people at my church put up with my ramblings once a month, which gives me a wonderful outlet for the words that Jesus keeps putting into my head. Through these writings I can tell others about a Savior who rescued me from a life that was, in reality, lifeless. In spite of my rebellious attitude, Jesus kept loving, accepting, and forgiving me. He will do that for you too.

This does not mean you will not have troubles, but it does mean you will be able to withstand them when Jesus is shouldering the load.

All of my rowdy friends have faced many of life's serious problems and are doing so still. Our faith in God is what enables us to see humor in situations and put things into the right perspective.

Jesus tells us in John 14:1-2, *"Let not your heart be troubled; you believe in God, believe also in Me.... I go to prepare a place for you."*

You – includes YOU!

CHANGE IN AN EVER CHANGING WORLD

"But everything exposed by the light becomes visible, for it is light that makes everything visible. This is why it is said: Wake up O sleeper, rise from the dead, and Christ will shine on you." Ephesians 5:13-14

We are a product of our upbringing along with our experiences. How do we recognize when our beliefs are interfering with what God would have us do to reach those who don't know about Him?

Take, for instance, the traditional Christian churches of yesterday; most would say *no* to men wearing a hat in church, but *yes* to women. In most Christian churches today, both sexes tend to wear no hats. Now, that is different from a Jewish synagogue, where it is *yes* for men to have on a hat, or a little beanie called a Kippa or Yarmulke. As far as I know, the women may or may not wear a scarf like covering for their heads. The pictures I've seen of men in Christ's day show all their heads covered while they were in the temple as well as the women in the courtyard.

There is a lot to be said for respecting a church sanctuary and dressing appropriately for meeting with God in His holy house. As a mature, Christian I understand this and feel comfortable when I am in this environment. Even though it was a product of my upbringing, I have no trouble today with someone coming to church in jeans or casual attire. It is their respect for our Lord Jesus that concerns me, not what they are wearing.

But what exactly does dressing appropriately entail? Take a simple thing like a man wearing a toque in church: what would you do if he wore one into your church?

We had this happen in our church after our Associate Pastor had worked very hard with a young man to get him to come to a church service. We had a middle-aged gentleman who was attending our church at the time come up to him and tell him to remove his toque in respect for God's house. Needless to say the young man was very embarrassed and upset, and after the service vowed to never set foot in our church again. When I heard about this, I prayed that it would not keep him from turning his life over to Jesus and seeking another church that would accept him as he was. Needless to say our Associate Pastor was devastated, and it wasn't long before he moved on and our church went through a split. Of course, the middle-aged gentleman who had created this dissension moved to another church as well.

If, in our zeal of good intentions to do what we deem is pleasing to God, we in reality alienate someone from Jesus, how would that action endear us to our loving Savior who gave His life for that young man? Before we act hastily, we should ask ourselves, *'What would Jesus do'?*

Many of today's youths, most of whom have never been in a church, know nothing about Jesus, let alone what clothing is appropriate to wear even to functions they attend outside the church. I find it very difficult to put myself in the place of today's young people since their parents have totally opted out of the responsibility to teach what I was taught as a child.

Jesus was merciful to us, so why should we not extend this same mercy, as well as the time He gave us to learn about Him, to others? If I have learned anything from Scripture, it tells me not to be righteously judgmental, but loving and kind and understanding, especially to the ones who are hard to love, and being human we all struggle with this problem.

We are taught in 1 Corinthians 13:4-8 that . . .

"Love is patient, love is kind. It does not envy, it does not boast, it is not proud. It is not rude, it is not self-seeking, it is not easily angered, and it keeps no record of wrongs. Love does not delight in evil but rejoices with the truth. It always protects, always trusts, always hopes, always perseveres. Love never fails..."

No matter who comes through our church doors, whether wearing a hat; old ragged dirty clothes; rings in their noses, eyebrows or else-where; red, blue or green hair *(remember when some older ladies used to love blue hair?)*; holey jeans (not to be confused with Holy Genes) or Dreadlocks. My very loving, 'born-again' grandson has these, and I told him I dread his dreadlocks, which gave us both a good laugh. However, that does not stop me from loving his kind, gentle soul because his hair isn't to my liking. I could go on, but you get the picture.

God takes us the way we are and gives us the opportunity to tell others about His forgiving love. But maybe more than that, He gives *us* the opportunity to *show them* His love through our actions and concern for their well-being. As the old saying goes: *"Actions speak louder than words."*

We must lovingly receive all who come through our church doors as well as our own doors. We don't know the life they have lived nor the pain they have suffered. Do not be the one to inflict more suffering upon them. For if Jesus taught us anything from the Scripture above, it is that He loves and accepts us right where we are today.

Being uncomfortable in these situations may be a good thing since it keeps us from getting used to the status quo, and it forces us to deal with change in this ever-changing world.

If we live 1 Corinthians, then many others who hear will want to know more about this Savior of hope. This opens the door for the Holy Spirit to bring them to a state of repentance, peace, and everlasting life.

STRENGTH OF FAITH

"Faith looks across the storm — it does not doubt or stop to look at clouds and things without. Faith does not question why when all His ways are hard to understand, but trusts and prays." Anon.

Have you ever thanked God ahead of time for something that is an impossibility under your present circumstances? You have little or no money — just skimming by — and yet you fully expect the Lord to come through. You reason, *"He is God, and He can do the impossible."*

Well for six months, my sister Maxine had been praying daily, *"Thank you, Lord, I'm so happy and grateful that you are giving me a house that is so well suited for me."*

This idea was somewhat foreign to me and seemed so bold as to presume that God had an obligation to supply such a request. Not even a request but, in my mind, a materialistic expectation.

Let me tell you a little about my sister, Maxine. She spent five years in Guyana as a Missioner with the Catholic Church. The first part of her years there she was in the Plains with heat and humidity. The last part she spent in the Mountains with the cold and dampness, where she developed Typhoid fever, forcing her to return home to Canada.

She lived the following two years in Niagara Falls, Ontario, with an income of the old age pension. In her sixties, she had to get a job to supplement her income.

The first year home she worked as a housekeeper-cook for an elderly, disagreeable gentleman, for little pay and even less thanks. The last year, she supplemented her income by sewing. All the while her rent on her small one bedroom apartment continued to climb, taking up more than half her monthly income. Through all this, she showed a joyful, positive attitude, fully believing God was going to give her a house that she could afford.

As children, Maxine and I fought like cats and dogs, and at one point in our childhood, she was so angry with me she stuck a pair of scissors in my head. I'm sorry to say that I brought her to that frustrated level. The only reason I mention it now is because it shows how our viewpoints often clashed. Fortunately as adults, we both make a big effort at being more understanding of each other's point of view and love each other dearly.

Maxine is only seventeen months younger than I am, and I can't imagine going out to find a job in my retirement years. Not that I don't work hard or know how to work, but I just do not have the same stamina to do what needs to be done out in the marketplace.

In my search to understand Maxine's prayer, there were four Biblical things I knew for sure:

1) Nothing I do in my Good Works can come close to payment for Christ's sacrifice.
2) I must labor every day and do so happily as unto the Lord.
3) I must trust in God with all my heart, soul, mind and strength.
4) I must have faith even the size of a mustard seed.

I know all this in my head, but what am I missing here? If I know all this, why do I think God would not want to give Maxine, or even me, good things? Why do I feel it is improper to thank Him for something I have need of ahead of time, waiting for Him to fulfill His promise? His words teach me: *"I tell you the truth, if you have faith and do not doubt... you will receive whatever you ask for in prayer."* Where then is my faith? Obviously, my mustard seed is of an abnormally small size.

Perhaps my problem is in my belief that I am unworthy of any such a gift. This means I am not living in Jesus' power as one of His children, but still as a sinner only drawing from my own power. I must feel undeserving of such love, such gifts from my Savior who has told me He loves me unconditionally. Jesus words to all His Saints are, *"Ask and it shall be given unto you"* when the asking is to glorify Him. Maxine believes this miracle will happen because she faithfully trusts in Jesus' word, which brings glory to Him as the giver of all good things.

My sister Joanna and brother-in-law Ray live eleven hours north of me on the shores of Lake Superior. Maxine, Neil and I had planned on visiting them for a couple of weeks in July of that year because Joanna had been working hard on God's behalf looking for a home for Maxine.

Because of Maxine's meager savings, low income, and the cost of housing in this present economy, the words that still came to my mind were... impossible, improbable, unlikely, doubtful, as well as... contrary to all reasonable expectations. My skepticism, however, was fading away as my eyes were being opened to how Jesus was working in and through all of us to fulfill Maxine's prayer.

We arrived in Rossport, Joanna and Ray's hometown at the time, on June 30th. The next day, July 1st, we went to see the first house Joanna had set up with a Realtor for our viewing. This home was a twenty minute ride to the nearby town of Terrace Bay.

This town was struggling to survive with the recent and possibly permanent closure of the pulp and paper mill. Many workers had left to find jobs elsewhere, leaving many homes vacant at astonishingly low prices.

The town had much to offer with their many services, library and hospital, breathtaking landscapes, and the infinite beauty of Lake Superior.

Canada Day, 2009, was a day we will always remember in Reverent Awe! Maxine looked at this home we went to view, considered all the costs, put in an offer she could afford, negotiated for a time or two, and presto, within a few short hours, had bought herself a home at a price that left our mouths hanging open in awe!

Satan however was not happy with our praises and thanks to God and began to throw a wrench into our ecstatic gears. On the following day when Maxine went to get insurance for her new home, she was told the oil tank was too old and had to be replaced. A further misunderstanding developed as the owners thought Maxine should pay half the cost. So at this point, she had to back out of the deal, as she did not have the extra money.

With a heavy questioning heart we began the chore of looking at other homes. Why had God shown us the perfect home and then taken it away? It was a very low point for all involved.

The sunshine reappeared a few days later when the owners came back after having realized the certificate they had was not appropriate for the tank and therefore was not acceptable to the Insurance company. They agreed to pay the full cost of replacement for the new tank, and asked if Maxine would reconsider buying the home. Reconsider?

Let me tell you a little about this home while you keep in mind that God does not do things in small measures. This home is situated on close to an acre of a beautifully landscaped lot with flowering trees, flower gardens, fenced in vegetable garden, paved drive, two car garage with a workshop in the back.

The house itself is a story and a half, all newly vinyl clad, new windows, three bedrooms, two baths, living/dining combination, large bright kitchen, two entrance porches with closets, full basement with laundry, new oil furnace, sauna with shower, cold room for fruits and vegetables, and a work room.

Also included in the sale was a stove with a self-cleaning oven, large fridge, dishwasher, washer and dryer, and a good size floor freezer, all in working condition which helped Maxine out tremendously as she did not have the money to purchase these items.

The owners also left a kitchen table, a sofa and matching chair in good condition, large older color TV with a DVD/VCR player. All the closets had shelving and the bedroom on the main floor made a perfect sewing room to help Maxine supplement her income when needed.

Outside a large wooden picnic table was left, along with a wooden swing that the owner had made, both painted a bright cheerful yellow, sitting on the cement patio.

Now this is where I tell you to grab your hat in awe at God's fabulous gift for Maxine as she got all of this for under $40,000. Man's gifts can never compare to God's gifts.

Through complete faith in Him all things are possible, probable, plausible but still— contrary to all reasonable expectations.

DISCOURAGEMENT

"Look, the Lord your God has set the land before you; go up and possess it, as the Lord God of your fathers has spoken to you; do not fear or be discouraged." Deuteronomy 1:21

I was chatting with Ted, a fellow writer, whose work I often include in my monthly EncouraGem Bulletin at church and on line. We were lamenting the fact that some Christians go around with a constant frown on their faces like the weight of the world is on their shoulders. I said to Ted, *"Where is their joy in the Lord? Why aren't they filled with enthusiasm and laughter for what He has done for them?"*

Ted replied with, *"Yes, I think you should rename your EncouraGem... DiscouraGem!"* I laughed as he fired off more one-liners, and as he was doing so, the idea was born in my mind for my next article to look through the eyes of a joyless Christian. So all you joyless Christians out there prepare to crack a smile, a chuckle maybe—I'll settle for a nod.

Dear God:

I have a problem. Well, it's not me exactly; it's those religious nuts in our church. They keep talking about spiritual fruit? They drone on and on about love, joy, peace, long-suffering (boy do I know about that), on and on about kindness, goodness, faithfulness, and gentleness. Why don't they get some self-control?

I realize that my growing old is inevitable; all I have to do is look in the mirror, but they seem to think growing old is something to be happy about. They say silly things like, "it only puts me one day closer to heaven." I'm so tired of their cheerful, unrealistic attitude about life.

Oh Lord, don't get me wrong; they are not malicious in any way, just always smiling and laughing when they should be acting sober and more mature and sedate. After all, this is a church, and they are showing such a poor example to the rest of the congregation.

They seem to have the impression they have the key to happiness, telling others your door is always open. Well that may be true of you, but the church doors are not always open. Our pastors have to sleep sometime, so I'm told.

Another thing, they go on and on about asking, seeking, finding, knocking. I'd like to give them a knock or two. I wish they would just be silent and hold their tongues, but noooo— they just go around so joyful and happy that it gets so discouraging. Don't they know how tough life is? Another problem is their belief, which is unbelievable. They say if they just had enough faith they could move a mountain. Can you believe the ego?

I know you tell us not to worry, but I just can't help worrying about our church and the way things are progressing. Who knows what these crazies will be changing next? All I see is the word 'trouble' when they enter a room. I am so anxious about them that I can't even pray, let alone smile when I meet them.

I'm doing the best I can Lord to avoid any contact with them, and you know how flexible I am, which makes it so difficult. I know I shouldn't carry a grudge, but this problem has me so nerved up.

Perhaps you might help me find a peaceful spot where I can unwind from all this levity, and get down to the serious problems of the world. You certainly know how many there are, which is no laughing matter to You.

I have one request though: could you help me out here by doing something to reach these people before they infect the whole congregation?

Yours in bondage,
Burdened.

YOUR ATTITUDE

"Your attitude should be the same as that of Christ Jesus who, being in very nature God, did not consider equality with God something to be grasped, but made Himself nothing, taking the very nature of a servant, being made in human likeness." Philippians 2:5-7

The word 'servant' is not considered an honorable thing in today's world. In fact, those who serve are often looked upon by the masses as inferior or ignorant.

The passage above in Philippians requires a necessary change in one's attitude toward life. This would be from an attitude of bemoaning a chore to eventually one of praising God for the privilege of being able to do it for Him.

A hypothetical example: Let's say I was enjoying fellowship with a group of people but had given my word that I would help out by participating in another commitment at the same time. I am enjoying myself so much that the thought enters my mind. *"Should I linger a little while longer? After all, my next commitment is not that important and can wait."*

Or sometimes thoughts will creep into your mind like, *"I give so much all the time. This is just another chore being loaded onto my already sagging shoulders. I know all that's required, so I don't really need to be there right yet. This is a poor use of my talents. This is not really part of my job. I am so tired of all these constant needs. I can quickly grasp what I need to do, so I can stay a while longer."* And on and on I might go, talking myself into procrastinating on that commitment.

Now, how do you think that attitude would come across to others who were counting on you to do what you said you would do? One thing is for certain; you would be setting yourself apart from those involved by indirectly telling them that you had more on your shoulders than they had on theirs. You would be, and rightfully so, viewed as part of the problem not part of the solution. You would also show a lack of caring for other people's time, as well as their well being.

If you are feeling put upon by others, perhaps it is because you have agreed to take on more work than you are able to handle, or else you are managing your time incorrectly.

When I memorized this passage of Scripture the words *your attitude* returned to me every time I began to moan and groan about the demands on my time.

Slowly but steadily I began to change my attitude, and when that Scripture popped into my mind I would work to see the job through Jesus' eyes as being a privilege to serve. This change began to bring me unexpected blessings.

To begin with, my attitude changed from one of duty to one of privilege. Harmony replaced discord with others in my life. I was no longer a burden to others around me as we worked happily together to get the job done. Action replaced my inaction. When asked to participate in helping out, I looked carefully at all my commitments before giving an answer. If I could not give it the time and attention required I told them sorry but not at that time.

Following Jesus into servanthood brought me peace and joy as He lifted the weight off my shoulders and pointed me in the direction that He wanted me to serve.

Tell me: do you feel overburdened, used, put upon, your talents wasted? Perhaps you too need a change in attitude along with a prioritizing of your time. Go to Jesus in prayer for the answers you are needing.

I love the Mercy Me song *'Here Am I'* from their album *'Almost There.'* The chorus goes,

Whom shall I send, Who will go for me, To the ends of the earth, Who will rise up for the King? Here am I... send me, Here am I... send me!

Perhaps you have never said these words for fear of being taken up on them. I urge you to pray for direction, and then step out in obedience when God says go.

I also urge you to memorize *Philippians 2:5-11*. It will have a positive, life-changing effect on your attitude.

MY WAY OR GOD'S WAY

I know not by what methods rare
The Lord provides for me;
I only know that all my needs
He meets so graciously. Adams

I've been thinking lately, *"What has Jesus done for me in my lifetime that I would let Him steer my course? Why have I put my trust in Him for answers?"* Many answers to those questions came floating into my mind like growing up with family-oriented parents who taught me Christian values through their actions and love; God blessing me with a best friend who led me to a Bible believing church; My faithful and loving husband; Four wonderful children and twelve loving grandchildren; along with many more answers too numerous to list. These were all certainly reasons enough for me to trust Him, but is that the only reason I trust in Jesus, because He gives me good things?

God blesses all people with good things, but as my life has shown, a good beginning does not mean I appreciated or recognized those gifts. Nor did it mean that I could not be led astray by my own headstrong decisions in following the wrong path or leader. We are all given choices and because we live in a fallen world, stumbling blocks are placed in all our paths. We have been given the choice of which path we will choose to follow. God does not want us to worship Him because He demands us to; if that was the case, all He needed to do was create robots.

Staying married for over fifty-four years does not mean I never experienced difficult marital problems. Many troubles arise while raising children to adulthood, and I can tell you from experience it was certainly no piece of cake. Going through serious health problems with my husband, me, and other loved ones brought many tough times into my life.

My periods of following occult practices, and doing things selfishly my way brought much pain into my life. But at that time I still reasoned, *"I am the master of my destiny, and I am in total control,"* even though the reality of each situation told me the only control I had was in the very choices I was making.

My marriage came closest to divorce during our years in the Resort business. We were so exhausted from the work demands that too many days ended in screaming matches of blame against each other. After all, one had to put on a smiling face to the public, leaving no one else to transfer our frustrations to except one another.

The reality of my choices manifested themselves through outbursts of temper tantrums towards my children and sometimes family or friends. There were times I physically lashed out or spewed venomous words that hit their mark with devastating accuracy. I realized later that only by the grace of God did I not inflict any long lasting physical or mental harm. Others sincerely forgave me for my outbursts, which was a miracle in itself.

Well, doing things my way eventually led me into times of depression and despondency. I thought at the time, *"If I just had everything fall into line the way I wanted it to line up, then my life would be wonderful."*

Lysa TerKeurst, in her article *'Coming Unglued Isn't All Bad,'* says this:

"Therefore, might we agree that coming unglued isn't all bad if it brings us to God? And brings to the light what is eating away at us – chipping away at our foundation? Coming unglued is glorious if the end result of that brokenness leads us to a more healthy wholeness."

A healthy wholeness began to take shape in my life when my eldest son Tim and his wife Donna, who were partners with us in the Housekeeping Resort we ran together, encouraged me to attend church as well as a women's weekly Bible study.

It was during this time that I began to remember the peace and joy I felt years before when I first met Jesus. I began to wonder what Jesus saw in me so many years ago. Who was that person then, and who had she become now?

How did Jesus feel about my disobedient spirit? I wanted to pray in the same way that Jesus prayed. I wanted to use the Holy Spirit's power within me to help me overcome all my problems. I wanted to be able to forgive others for their shortcomings as Jesus had forgiven me for mine.

Slowly I began to see my husband through new and more loving eyes. We talked about our lashing out at each other and decided that we would not verbally abuse and blame each other for what was being thrown our way by circumstances beyond our control. It took a lot of tongue biting, but we persevered and overcame as our marriage grew stronger. A wonderful side effect to that decision was the rekindling of our faith in God.

My depression, anger, frustrations, bitterness, emptiness, selfishness, and envy were replaced with the fruits of the Spirit: love, joy, peace, long-suffering, kindness, goodness, faithfulness, gentleness, and self-control.

All these things did not suddenly drop into my lap at one time, but as I began earnest Bible study, prayed for strength and guidance, and memorized Scripture, all those destructive feelings and behaviors were replaced with a peace and love I had not experienced in years. Doing things my way was not my answer anymore; I looked forward to doing things Jesus way.

Since that time, difficulties have not disappeared from my life, especially these last few years with the loss of my husband, my own health problems, and those of my family.

It's been difficult to learn how to live as a single person after so many years of making decisions together for all the problems of running a home. However I can say unequivocally that without Jesus in my life, I would still be an anxious, depressed, unhappy mess.

Since my renewed faith, I am now able to see what Jesus sees when He looks at me and at other hurting people; after all, I was one of them that He lovingly restored.

Answers to my problems readily become available to me when I turn to Him in prayer and continue to study His words. He encourages me to look away from myself and see others who are struggling. I can now show them through my loving actions the way I found true peace and healing.

So you see there are many reasons I have put my trust in Jesus to guide my life. He has never let me down; instead He always encouraged me to trust Him to lead me through the mazes of my life. He is right there ready to take away my burdens while encouraging me to take the next step.

Have you been searching for answers through the same avenues I chose or similar ones? The occult and other religions including some who call themselves Christians will tell you that you can do it on your own, that you are your own god in total control over your own destiny.

Take it from one who has been there: only belief in Jesus as the One and Only Son of God can bring an everlasting peace and joy to your soul.

"Therefore do not let sin reign in your mortal body so that you obey its evil desires. Do not offer any part of yourself to sin as an instrument of wickedness, but rather offer yourselves to God as those who have been brought from death to life: and offer every part of yourself to him as an instrument of righteousness." Romans 6:12-13

NO SHOTS FIRED

"The end of a matter is better than it's beginning, and patience is better than pride."
Ecclesiastes 7:8

Hunting season was upon us and taken very seriously by some while completely ignored by others. Take Neil and me for instance: the only 'wild game' we ever killed were mice or other rodents, and that by trap or poison. I am not adverse to other people hunting, and I certainly have never said *"no, thank you"* to a generous or sharing friend.

I now live in town where my house is mouse-proof unless I leave a door open, but thankfully that has not happened. In the past when I found one in a trap, the first thing I did was shiver all over, then call for Neil to come to remove the poor beastie. At that point, I gave strict instructions *NOT* to dispose of it in the kitchen garbage.

When we lived in the country, the deer around our house knew we were putty in their little hoofs. They loved to come into our yard to eat the apples, flowers, cedar trees (often whole sides in a tough winter), grass, and whatever else took their fancy. No matter what we did, they munched on. Now that I live in town you would think my garden would be safe, but deer still love to come down through a forest area behind the row of houses across the street and eat my Hostas, as well as chomping off some of the buds of my other flowers before I even get to oooh or aaah.

The only threat the deer had around our house back then was from our little black Schipperke dog (pronounced Skipperkee), Mighty Max. She was one foot high and weighed fifteen pounds, a Belgian breed that was bred to kill rats on ships. When she was a pup she had an excellent trainer, and the majority of time she would do everything we asked of her.

However, Max was one sweet dog with one huge flaw. In her mind she believed she was the size of a Great Dane. This delusion would have her running up to anything one hundred times her size to bite them on the nose as many times as she possibly could manage. When her focus was on a giant invading her domain, she thought of nothing else but attack!

She did this once with a big Rottweiler, biting it not once but four times on the nose. Of course this incensed giant retaliated by grabbing her by the neck, ready to end her existence in one snap. Fortunately, Jim was there and his quick action saved the day by swiftly bringing his foot up under the big dog's belly. With that well-placed kick, the big dog reacted by opening his mouth, thus dropping Max in the bargain.

During one hunting season in November, Neil and I were about to leave on a trip to Toronto when we came to a stop at the end of our driveway. A vehicle had hit a deer and the entrails and offal were strewn around and across its belly. Offal is well named, as it sure was awful. Needless to say the deer was dead so we dragged it as best we could to the edge of the drive so we could get out.

Neil went back into the house and phoned the Ministry of Natural Resources. The gentleman answering the phone said that since it was hunting season he was up to his eyeballs in paperwork, but he would try to get it removed by Monday. He asked Neil if he wanted the meat, but Neil said no because it appeared to him that rigor mortis had already set in, and he didn't think road kill was safe to eat.

We thought of phoning our friend Bryan to confirm this, but he was off at his camp hunting. It turns out he shot three deer at that time all by himself. However, we got ours without firing a shot. Unfortunately, ours wasn't edible.

Well, Monday came and went, Tuesday, Wednesday, Thursday, and no MNR. By this time the other birds and beasties had discovered the rotting carcass and missing was a tongue, an eyeball, plus other things too unmentionable to mention.

On Friday Neil called the MNR again, chatting with the same fellow. Neil explained that there might be a health hazard breeding at the end of our driveway. The fellow said he was having a hectic time chasing after all the bad hunters who were shooting on private property. He asked Neil if he would be able to drag the carcass away from the driveway to let nature continue to take its course? Neil agreed to try.

The next day we managed to tie a rope around the carcass's rotting neck, and with both of us laboriously tugging and pulling, managed to haul it a good distance up the road. Once there we were able to push it into the ditch well away from our home or anyone else's home.

Now, all the while we were doing this, Mighty Max was on the other side of our chain-link fence making a terrible racket barking and growling as we dragged away. At this point we were not only tired from hauling the rotting deer, but our patience was running very thin with Max ignoring our shouts of (to put it nicely), *"cease and desist!"* If God had turned her into a pillar of salt at that moment, it would have been okay with us.

It was a long time afterward before we saw any more deer around our house. However that didn't stop delusional Mighty Max, as she sat proudly on our verandah surveying her kingdom. She continued to chase anything that dared to invade her domain. In her mind, she was the one who had rid her land of that dastardly deer and would do the same to any others that dared to cross her territory.

As for me I kept looking out my window longingly, saying, *"Please come back little Bambi..nos."* In case you didn't know it — that's Italian for deer.

IF JESUS CAME TO YOUR CHURCH

"And while they went to buy, the bridegroom came, and those who were ready went in with him to the wedding; and the door was shut. Afterwards the other virgins came also, saying, 'Lord, Lord, open to us!' But He answered and said, 'Assuredly, I say to you, I do not know you.'" Matthew 25:10-12

Most of us have heard the poem 'If Jesus came to your House,' but what about changing that to 'If Jesus came to your church'? In this modern day, what would be the reaction of those of us sitting in the pews if Jesus really did show up in our church?

Do you think we would have our cell phones out, texting or playing the latest game? Would we care about the clothes we wore, thinking we were not as nicely dressed as the person sitting next to us? Would we have to down an aspirin because we stayed up too late partying the night before? Would we be indifferent to what He was saying because our mind was filled with the cares of the past week and worries about what lies lurking for us in the week to come?

Perhaps you would think to yourself, *"I've heard this all before and it's the same old, same old,"* so you would close your eyes, stifle a yawn, and try to keep from drifting off for a little nap. Or would you stare blankly ahead, putting on a mask of interest while feeling bored and *"like I want to be anywhere else but here, man"*?

Maybe you're irritated because you feel the songs are too modern, or your irritation grows because you liken the hymns to the time of Columbus? And you certainly don't want to shake hands with anybody with all those horrid germs floating around. And on and on it might go.

But perhaps your reaction would be different if you had the privilege of Jesus coming to your Church. Instead of being bored you would find yourself hanging on His every word, so eager to know everything about Him. You would long to sing the hymns—whether old or new, with joy and enthusiasm, knowing you are singing to your Savior. You would feel the Holy Spirit in each and every word, just as the composer felt when he or she put pen to paper.

You might have a new interest in listening to the *"same old, same old"* stories, with a new understanding of how they do truly apply to your life. You may not even think about the clothes you are wearing; or what the newest computer game is; which boy, girl, friend, foe said what to hurt your feelings.

Instead you would fall down on your knees with your face to the ground and worship Jesus in a way you have never worshiped Him before. You would be filled with thanksgiving for what He has sacrificed for you as you lift your hands and hearts in reverent prayer to Him.

Well, do you want to know a secret? Jesus *does* come to your church: every time you show up, He is there! He is listening to you while you sing, praise, and worship Him. He is there when you hear His words preached through the very people He has chosen to teach you all about Himself. He is there to welcome and encourage you along with all of His other children that He has purposely placed around you.

Jesus wants you to come and meet with Him at His church so He can bless you in a way you have never experienced before.

Listen — hear Him calling your name — speaking softly in your ear — telling you how very much He loves you — strengthening you through all your doubts and fears.

I guarantee you will come away rejuvenated in mind, body and soul as you discover that Jesus is right now waiting for you at your church. Won't you join Him there?

LET ME TRUST IN YOU LORD

Let me trust in you Lord
In all I do and say,
Wherever I may wander
Instil in me your ways.

Let me trust in you Lord
As each new day arrives
In morning light
Your words delight
My soul becomes alive.

Let me trust in you Lord
As your stories are retold
In generations old and new,
Keep me loyal, faithful, bold.

Let me trust in you Lord
With purpose as I trod
O'er streets that are paved
In fields ripe with grain
Let me rest in your work on the cross.

THE BIBLE BANNED, BURNED, BELOVED

"But they mocked God's messengers, despised his words and scoffed at his prophets until the wrath of the Lord was aroused against his people and there was no remedy." 2 Chronicles 36:16

Conflicting opinions abound, along with confusion about whom God really is, as well as what the Bible tells us about Him. How has God loved us, people ask? If God really loved us, He would never allow wars, sickness or death.

Some believe God loves us no matter what we do or how we live. After all, they state,

"If He is a God of love like the Bible tells us, and we really are not bad like some people

we know or see on the nightly news, that is all that's needed to get to heaven."

Some people believe the Bible is part myth, part allegory, with some truth in the mix. Then there are those who don't believe it at all, and vehemently try to discredit its worth. Some have never read one word of it, but still spout an opinion on its meaning and content.

The Bible is today—as it has been in the past — banned, burned or beloved.

It has been more widely read and more frequently attacked than any other manuscript. The Bible still outsells every bestseller, is translated into more languages than any other book, and has even been carried to the moon. No other book in history has its endurance record.

Chuck Colson stated in his book, Loving God,

"Literary classics endure; Philosophers mold the thoughts of generations; modern media shape current culture; yet nothing has affected the rise and fall of civilization, the character of cultures, the structure of governments, or

the lives of this planet, as profoundly as the words of the Bible."

So what does the Bible tell us about God?

It begins by telling us that He is the creator of the heavens and the earth and mankind. Now, you would think we would be grateful for that, but look around you and ask people who He is and what they know about Him. Today, many people have not heard the name Jesus Christ except as a swear word.

As we read *Psalm 146:8*, we notice that God loves the humble and the righteous:

"The Lord opens the eyes of the blind; The Lord raises those who are bowed down; The Lord loves the righteous." It also tells us in Psalm 145:20 that He hates wickedness: "The Lord preserves all who love Him, but all the wicked He will destroy."

Destroy? Where is His love for us here? Well Ephesians 2:4-7 explains,

"But God, who is rich in mercy, because of His great love with which He loved us, even

when we were dead in trespasses, made us alive together with Christ."

Delving further into the New Testament, we begin to realize just how much Jesus suffered because of His love for us:

"For God so loved the world that He gave His one and only Son, that whoever believes in Him shall not perish but have eternal life" (John 3:16).

"In this is love, not that we loved God, but that He loved us and sent His Son to be an atoning sacrifice for our sins" (1 John 4:10).

Did you read that? God the Father sacrificed His own Son so we could have the very choice of personally accepting or rejecting Him.

Zephaniah 3:17 in the Old Testament further explains God's love for us:

"The Lord your God in your midst, The Mighty One, will save; He will rejoice over you with

gladness. He will quiet you with His love, He will rejoice over you with singing."

Rejoice over someone who has done nothing but malign and spew hatred for Him?

Considering all these things, God's love is not only amazing, but also very different from the world's definition of love. Here is a glimpse into what God has in store for those who love Him:

"But as it is written: No eye has seen, no ear has heard, no mind has conceived, what God has prepared for those who love Him" 1 Corinthians 2:9.

Throughout the ages, the Bible has told us:

"The Lord has appeared of old to me, saying: 'Yes, I have loved you with an everlasting love; Therefore with loving kindness I have drawn you'" Jeremiah 31:3.

God's love for us is unconditional and will last forever.

I have given you a small glimpse into what the Bible has to offer to you, but I encourage you to search it out by getting a Bible and reading it for yourself.

A. W. Tozer says it so well in his book 'The Pursuit of God.' —

"I think a new world will arise out of the religious mists when we approach our Bible with the idea that it is not only a book which was once spoken, but a book which is now speaking. The prophets habitually said, 'Thus saith the Lord.' They meant their hearers to understand that God's speaking is in the continuous present."

WHICH FILE OR PILE

"All the days of the oppressed are wretched, but the cheerful heart has a continual feast."
Proverbs 15:15

Failing is part of coping in this fallen world, but we are supposed to learn from our failures. However, there are some things that seem to take some people forever to learn, no matter how hard they try.

Take me, for instance. A few years back *(well... quite a few)*, I attended Business College and passed all my courses with good standing. That is, all but one! Seems I had trouble grasping this subject back then, and I still have a problem with it to this day. I have improved over the years, but for the amount of time and energy I have given to overcome this failure, I really should be acing this subject, not crawling up to a pass.

I will come right out with it and tell you that... *I FAILED FILING.*

I know, I know, *"How can anyone fail filing?"* you say. Well, it seems to come quite easily to me.

I keep a fairly neat and tidy home, no problem there. I can organize my cupboards, closets, dinner parties, rooms, children, my blog, the Internet, computers *(I love electronic gadgets),* and the like, but when it comes to filing, I completely and utterly fail.

Also, I was—and am constantly to this day—searching for pieces of paper. They are often small, as I grab any bit of paper upon which I can scribble some important piece of information. The information I am seeking could also be in one of my many scribblers. It could also be a big piece of paper that I have filed, but cannot remember under which file or pile that I filed it???

I have literally piles of valuable *(valuable to me)* information heaped here and there, as well as in filing cabinets to call upon at the appropriate time that God brings it to my attention. Unfortunately, I always end up with the same old question rearing its ugly head: *"Which File or Pile?"* And so the searching begins.

Computers give me nominal success, but I still must remember not only what name I used to file the document, but also the name of the document.

One reason I have better success with computers is that I don't use them for all the little notes or papers, so it is easier to browse through files looking for names that may provide a clue.

Long ago I thought I had the perfect solution for this failing of mine. I had been using a large cardboard box in which to throw all these *'gems'* of encouragement. Finding anything in the box, though, was just adding to the problem, and it always took so much of my time.

I felt the solution would be to add another filing cabinet or two to my existing one. Along with this I would give the files new names so that I would be able to find what I needed quickly.

So I took myself to Zellers where I found two file cabinets that could be mounted on top of each other and put on wheeeeeels. That was great, as far as I was concerned. Not only could I organize my files, but also re-organize my office by easily wheeling the files around the room. To me they were the perfect solution, and so — I brought them home.

Enthused and confident that I was getting on top of my problem, I came up with what I hoped were appropriate labels and began to file the papers into my new file cabinets from my overflowing box.

I was happily working away when time, *as it usually does*, ran out on me. I still had a stack of papers to process, and it was now time to begin preparing my articles for the next edition of PANews (Pinegrove Action News).

During this time I had also been gathering more *'gems'* that held promise. My office now had new and old papers on my desk, table, bed, old filing cabinet, and new filing cabinets, file box, along with some papers that were thankfully crumpled up and thrown into the garbage.

The good news was I had all these papers in neat piles around the room ready to be filed under the new labels in the new filing cabinets. However, as I worked away the question remained the same as before I bought the cabinets, *"Now which file or pile?"*

Things haven't improved that much today. When I look around my present office I see piles of papers in, yes, a new cardboard box, a couple of new desk-top files, all filing cabinets, plus other files and piles throughout the closet, as well as in boxes under some desks, and on top of a desk.

I do take great comfort in 2 Corinthians 12:9, especially where it says, *"My power is made perfect in weakness."*

So Lord, take this weakness of mine and help me to step forward boldly so that You can once again try to teach this old dog a few new *(or old by now)* tricks.

I must say that I am still fully determined though *(as well as assured at this moment)* that I will eventually *pass filing*, hopefully before the Lord takes me home. Of course, after that it won't matter.

Lord, I know You have been over this with me many times before, but would you explain it once again? If I have an article with the title *'IMPOSTOR,'* under which letter of the alphabet should it be filed?

Oh Yes, of course! . . . *Under 'S' for 'SATAN' right?* I think I'm finally getting the hang of this.

PART THREE – HOMEWARD BOUND

LET THE SON SHINE IN

"Do not store up for yourselves treasures on earth, where moth and rust destroy, and where thieves break in and steal. But store up for yourselves treasures in Heaven, where moth and rust do not destroy, and where thieves do not break in and steal. For where your treasure is, there your heart will be also." Matthew 6:19-21

It has been such a beautiful spring this year — so different from the rainy, dull spring days of last year. I have a friend that I pay a modest sum to do my gardens, and she has our grounds looking so wonderful. All I need do is maintain them. And to this end, I have happily bought pots of annuals to add an extra splash of color amongst the perennials.

I set three pots of colorful Petunias *(Neil's favorite)* on our back deck for him to enjoy now that he is able to get outside. It has been such a long tedious and emotional winter for us with his health problems. It has brought much joy to us to once again see beauty and color splashed around the yard. Feeling the warmth from the sun is glorious indeed, while being able to walk outdoors without putting on layers of clothes brings a wonderful sense of freedom.

So while I was basking in this much sought-after atmosphere of freedom from a long winter, what do you suppose shows up in the mail? It was a notice that our copy of the Sears *winter* catalogue was awaiting our pick-up at the store.

Winter catalogue? I am still basking in the warmth of spring and looking forward to the heat of summer, and they want me to start thinking about winter again. Winter with its sweaters, coats, boots—cold, snowy, drab, dull and lifeless days indoor.

That is just like life, isn't it though? Here we are plodding along through problems and troubles, thinking the sun will never again peek through those overcast skies. But just as you are about to give up, a ray from the *'Son'* peeks through the gloom. The sky begins to clear and all the colors become vibrant and pleasing to the eye. You bask in the Son's rays that give you warmth and a lift of Vitamin D — Delicious, Dependable, Desirous, Doctrine of His Devotion.

As you are relaxing, the tempter of this world (you know who I mean) comes along saying *"Hey! Look over here. This Sonshine isn't going to last long, and you'd better hurry and get ready for the cold winter months ahead.*

But the Sonshine holds me fast. I refuse to jump ahead in time, preferring to enjoy the here and now.

The winter catalogue sits to the side. I haven't picked it up yet or even peeked at the first page. Perhaps in September I might take a glance or two, but in the meantime I thank you Jesus for this wonderful spring day that you have given us to share together.

HONESTLY HONEST

"The one who lives righteously and speaks rightly, who refuses gain from extortion, whose hand never takes a bribe, who stops his ears from listening to murderous plots and shuts his eyes to avoid endorsing evil—he will dwell on the heights; his refuge will be the rocky fortresses, his food provided, his water assured. Your eyes will see the King in His beauty; you will see a vast land." —Isaiah 33:15-17

"The trouble with you, Neil, is you're too honest for your own good."

Honestly, an influential chairwoman of the North York Board of Education said this to my husband because he refused to bend the rules for her. This was, of course, said privately during a closed-door meeting to try to coerce him to do things her way.

At this point, Neil was a Superintendent of Schools. He always had the children and teacher's best interests at heart, and he would never have jeopardized that responsibility for anything or anyone, no matter what the cost. And, of course, cost him it did.

Thwarting this woman's power struggle cost him many times because it prevented him from being able to accommodate the needs of the children and teachers. Sad to say, she was not the only one to think and act this way. Often he took a lone stand, but his integrity was always in tact.

I honestly could not believe how often Neil was bombarded or struck down by people trying to climb the world's ladder of success. Work was heaped upon his already sagging shoulders because they knew he would get it done. Well-earned promotions were delayed or passed him by entirely. Health problems began to rear their ugly heads from the stress. Yet God carried him through these difficult times by blessing him in so many tangible ways.

The men, women and children he helped along the way with their careers or their schooling loved and respected him. When they unexpectedly met him years later, they would tell him how he had helped them through a very difficult time or with a serious decision they had to make in their lives. They were so grateful to him for his caring about their well being. Neil was always surprised by this because he did not realize the impact that his honesty had had on others. But God knew, and these stories always brought him a blessing of encouragement.

The pupils' education was steeped in this man's honesty, and they knew from his actions and words that they could trust him. They were not afraid to show their love with happy smiles and big hugs. Teenagers wanted to be around him, eager to talk on any topic, savoring his advice as he took the time that each one needed. They went on in their schooling or into the work force armed with the *sword of truth*, even though they may not have known its Biblical roots.

When he was laid up by heart attacks he was showered with love and best wishes from his peers, friends, teachers, parents, children, and of course by his loving family and concerned relatives.

God brought him through these difficult times as he learned to depend more and more on the teachings of Christ that his mother had taught to him as a child.

Our family too grew closer to God as we stood stunned and helpless by Neil's side, trying to comprehend what our lives would be like without a husband and a father.

Our prayers for his healing were answered so many times over the years, until our prayers for his ultimate healing were answered that New Years Eve in 2010. Promotion did not pass him by at that time! He received the ultimate reward when Jesus took him home to heaven. That is when honesty is honestly the best policy.

Peter said it this way: *"As each one has received a special gift, employ it in serving one another."* *(1Peter 4:10)* Your greatest fulfillment in life will come when you discover your unique gifts and abilities and use them to edify others and glorify the Lord.

FISHERS OF MEN

"A servant of the Lord must not quarrel but be gentle to all, able to teach, patient." 2 Timothy 2:24

Have you ever told anyone about your deepest sins? The ones you want to remain between you and God? The ones you don't want your children, family or friends to know about? The ones you want to immediately push out of your mind because they bring you memories of a time when you were far away from the Lord? A time when you grieved the Holy Spirit but didn't care because you knew what was best for your life? Who needed Jesus: to see your future all you needed to do was read your horoscope.

We ended our Fresh Encounter Bible study with a lively discussion about being Fishers of Men. I asked, *"How can one be used of God in this way?"* This question was relevant to me because I felt I pushed more people away from Jesus than towards Him. I often would get the urge to grab them by the collar, give them a good shake, and say, *"Why can't you see this? I understood it when I was eleven years old."*

But did I understand it then? I accepted Jesus as my Savior at that time, but from my twenties on into my fifties, I lived life my way, the way of the world. Enjoying what was touted as the *Good Life* with my way being the only way of looking at anything. No wonder no one wanted to listen to more of my opinions. I had it wrong for years, and God had to send some very stern lessons my way to bring me back to the fold.

Not that I haven't had some success in telling others about Jesus' love for them. I was able to lead one of my grandsons to the Lord, as well as a friend who lay dying in a hospital bed. At the time, his son was skeptical and wondered, *"Did he really accept the Lord or was he too sick to tell you to leave?"* I believe he did accept Jesus that day from the joy on his face, and I felt the room fill with the Holy Spirit. I won't know for sure until I get to heaven.

Our discussion led to many suggestions, some of which I had already tried. Pastor Don said I should not lose heart, as there were many who walked away from his efforts to tell them about Jesus.

One of the ladies at Fresh Encounters said to me,

"Syb, you have a gift of writing. Why don't you write your testimony, and instead of getting into an argument, hand them your reasons to believe? They can read it at a later time when feelings have cooled down, and they are able to contemplate your words."

That was a very good idea, but I tackled her suggestion in a different way. I am writing about my experiences with Jesus, but what I hand out is my EncouraGem writings that God is using to reach more people than I could in my own little corner of the world.

As Jesus changes me and prepares me, He leads me through different doors as my fears of rejection evaporate away, and I keep my focus on Him.

He has gifted me with putting my failures into written words as the Holy Spirit brings them to my mind. He has reassured me with His words, *"I will never leave you nor forsake you" (Hebrews 13:5b),* as well as, *"For we are God's Handiwork, created in Christ Jesus to do Good Works, which God prepared in advance for us to do" (Ephesians 2:10).*

Arthur Christopher Benson wrote,

"No faith can have vitality or hope which does not hold that we are somehow the better for our failures and our falls, however much they have devastated our life and influence, with whatever shame and self-reproach they may have wasted our days."

The following poem seemed to say it so well for me —

O Lord, transform my stubborn heart
And help me always see
That gentle, kind, and courteous
Is what I ought to be. – Anon.

DISCIPLE OR APOSTLE

"Therefore go and make Disciples of all nations..... teaching them to obey everything I have commanded you." Matt.28:19-20

I always thought of Disciple and Apostle as one and the same because Jesus called the twelve by both names. Recently I began to think about that and focused on the definitions. I found that 'Disciple' means follower or learner—someone who follows another person submitting himself to the teaching of that person while 'Apostle' means messenger or missionary—a person sent with a special message.

Jesus' words according to Luke 6:13 states, *"He called his disciples to Himself; and from them He chose twelve whom He also named apostles."*

During the time that Jesus spent with them beforehand, they were His Disciples *(followers)* who were in the process of learning from His teachings. When Jesus sent them out to perform miracles, heal the sick, and tell others about Him, they were His Apostles *(messengers or missionaries)*. In today's words, evangelists, missionaries and preachers.

This encourages me because I know at this time in my life that I will never be a missionary or a preacher *(although some who know me may disagree about the latter)*, but I feel Jesus has equipped me to be a messenger of sorts, by the gifts He has bestowed upon me.

He has equipped me through my writings, through my loving actions towards others, through the soft and kind words that I speak, and through my daily prayers. All of these allow me to relay to others the message of His love, acceptance, and hope that they can have when they seek Him.

Of the many gifts the Lord has given me, my gift of writing has been my passion and brings me the most joy. Perhaps it is because I can organize my thoughts in such a way that my words are not offensive to the reader.

I believe my words are planted by the Holy Spirit to continue what He has prepared for the next person with the gifts required to finish the work that He has begun.

This burden was lifted from my shoulders when Pastor Don said to me, *"Perhaps you are a planter of the seed."* A planter? John 4:37 does tell me that *"one sows and another reaps."* Now, I can do that. I love to plant seeds, but I can't hoe much with this bad back of mine.

Sooo, what kind of seed do you want me to plant for You today, Lord?

Here's a question to ponder: *What kind of seed is Jesus asking you to plant today?*

NAME CALLING

Master, speak, and make me ready,
When Thy voice is truly heard,
With obedience glad and steady,
Still to follow every word.—Havergal

I awoke one morning with a start as I heard someone call my name. I was so sure about it that I partially sat up in bed and said out loud, *"Yes?"* After a moment I laid back down rather dazed, realizing that the voice I heard was in my head and not in my house.

I have had this happen before but never to the point of answering out loud. *"Perhaps I'm losing my grip on reality here,"* I thought to myself.

Neil lay in the bed next to mine still sound asleep, and it was one time I was happy about his hearing problem.

Now, I am sure most of us have had this kind of experience, although we may not go so far as to verbally answer out loud. I say most of us because I mentioned the incident to Neil at breakfast, and he said he has never had such a thing happen to him.

I must admit it left me with an odd sensation since it brought to my mind another in the Bible whose name was called, and he answered out loud three times. This led me to the question, *"What is the meaning of people's names?"*

Now, I don't liken myself to the prophet Samuel whom God called out of a sleep three times, and each time Samuel thought it was Eli calling him. Of course, once Eli realized it was God calling Samuel, he quickly put him on the right track.

However, I do believe that God was preparing me beforehand for this article when he woke me up at two in the morning a couple of nights later thinking about the incident and the words, *"What's in a person's name that identifies them to others?"* So I got up and began investigating my Bible for the answers.

For instance, in 1 Samuel 25 we find out that *'Nabal'* means *'fool'*, and from what the Bible tells us, he lived his name to the fullest by almost getting his household slaughtered when he drunkenly refused to give David and his men food. This, after David had protected Nabal's livestock and household for many months.

However, Nabal's wife, Abigail, saved the day by wisely and bravely averting the catastrophe. I encourage you to read it to find out how she accomplished that feat.

What really concerned me was, *"When someone calls my name, do they recognize me immediately as someone who knows and loves the Lord?"*

And more so, *"When **God** calls my name, can He trust me to listen and obey whatever it is He may be asking of me?"*

When my name is called by others, am I thought of as a generous, loving, kind, understanding, helpful, source of joy as was Abigail? How about as Lydia, who was a wise woman of commerce?

I love the story of Ruth in the Book of Ruth whose friendship and loyalty to her mom-in-law, Naomi, helped them overcome some very difficult circumstances together.

But I shudder to think that when my name is called the name *'Nabal—fool'* comes to people's minds.

What about you? When someone calls your name, what meaning do you think comes into his or her mind about you?

Would it be

Abigail–Source of joy
David–Beloved
Lydia–a maiden
Naomi–Pleasant
Ruth–companion, friendship
Samuel–God hears, heard by God
Or would it be . . . *Mara–Bitter*
Or worse yet . . . *Nabal–Fool, senseless*

WHAT LOVE

What Love . . .
A little babe in manger lay
Mother beside Him — with love did gaze
upon her babe in swaddling clothes
The Son of God – an angel disclosed.
What love
What faith
What gift divine
Sent from Heaven for all mankind.

What Love . . .
This willing Savior gave
so I could gaze upon that tree
that took Him at Calvary.
What love
given to set me free
from these earthly bonds —
He rescued me
What love.

*What Love . . .
Our Heavenly Father showed
when He turned His face
from this Son of Man —
His One and Only Son He gave.
Would I do the same
with a son of mine?
No . . .
I could not stand the pain
the stain
That evil inflicted upon my lamb
My precious lamb from God.*

*What Love . . .
I cannot comprehend.*

OLD BROOM-NEW BROOM

"....I will sweep her with the broom of destruction, declares the LORD Almighty."
Isaiah 14:23b

We have all seen what a new broom looks like. It has straight clean bristles to pick up the dirt while being attached to a long, strong, round wooden handle. All in all, a great instrument for its chosen profession.

Now compare that to the old broom that has had years of usage. It has stubby, dirty, bent-out-of-shape bristles, which means one has to go over and over the same area to get the dirt that a new broom would get in one sweep. I guess that is why the saying was born, *"A new broom sweeps clean."*

At one time the old broom was a new broom. When the old broom began as a new broom, it too was able to pick up piles of dirt with ease. Over and over the new broom cleaned faithfully day after day, month after month, year after year, until it became what it is today—worn down and worn out. What good is this old broom now?

To answer that question, we need to look at the differences in 'broom masters.' There are two types to choose from:

The first one cares about and looks after His broom. He keeps it dry and not left out in the elements that quickly wear away and destroy its effectiveness, strength, and use to the broom-master.

The second broom-master does not care about how he treats the broom. After all, it is just a broom, and he can replace it with another broom easily enough. So when the broom does not bring satisfaction to the broom-master anymore, there is only one thing for him to do—throw the old broom on the garbage heap or into the fire.

What about the broom's uses? The bristles receive the hardest wear; therefore it is usually the first part to wear down and wear out, but the old broom can be useful in places that are too dirty for a new broom. Broom handles are often usable long after the bristles are worn away. They can be re-attached to many other types of instruments that need a ready-made handle, or simply used as a doorstopper.

We all begin life like the new broom. Over the years, we wear down and wear out. The facts of life dictate that, in time, we will all be replaced by a new broom. However, the kind of broom-master we choose will make a big difference in how many more years we are useful to Him.

Long ago I choose to have a broom-master like the first One, a broom-master I can trust to look after me. When I am old and worn, unable to do the jobs I used to do, He will still find another use for me that will bring Him recognition for the good broom-master that He is. Because I put my trust in Him, He will not need to throw me on the garbage heap, or worse yet, into the unquenchable fire.

Discouragement and Dreams

*So many things in the line of duty
Drain us of effort and leave us no beauty,
And the dust of the soul grows thick and unswept,
The spirit is drenched in tears unwept.
But just as we fall beside the road,
Discouraged with life and bowed down with
our load,
We lift our eyes, and what seemed a dead end
Is the street of dreams where we meet a friend.
Helen Steiner Rice*

OLD BODY YOUNG EYES

"They will still bear fruit in old age, healthy and green, to declare: 'The Lord is just; He is my rock...'" Psalm 92:14-15

I have always been blessed with an abundance of energy. The normal pace for me has been more of a steady trot than a walk. People were always saying to me, *"Slow down, relax, take it easy."* But that has never been my body's pace.

My eyes see something that needs doing or that is going to create a problem, and my body jumps into high gear trying to correct the situation. I sometimes liken myself to a Martha, as it often distracts me from what is really needed at the time.

In the last couple of years, I have noticed a troubling change happening in my body. I have these young energetic eyes that has my brain convinced they belong in a young body.

Well, that is, until my young eyes look in a mirror, and I think, *"Who is this person? Why are you invading my body and sabotaging my trot?"* My old body sometimes balks and says to my young eyes, *"I quit,"* and completely runs out of fuel, even though I just refilled the tank.

Once in a while my old body states, *"Time to stop and rest,"* so I sit down in a chair and then, horror of horrors, a few times my old body has fallen asleep amid my thoughts of what my young eyes are itemizing needs doing. Much to my dismay, my old body is taking over more and more of my young eyes' previously owned territory.

But I have noticed an upside to this dilemma. The times that my old body forces me to rest have opened up some wonderful opportunities for me to listen and talk more with Jesus. It helps me to pay more attention to the problems of others around me. This gives me the opportunity to pray for them. That seems to satisfy my young eyes and old body at the same time.

Well, that is, until my mind says, *"All right, time to rock and roll!"* That's when my young eyes snap open and my old body feels young again, gung-ho to tag along with whatever work Jesus has set before me.

Now here's what I get from tagging along with Jesus:

* *Adventures of which I could never have dreamed or imagined.*
* *Gifts graciously endowed that I could never accomplish on my own.*
* *A heart overflowing with love for others—even those with whom I don't see eye to eye.*
* *A Joy unstoppable, unspeakable. I can't explain it. It is just there even in the down times.*
* *A glimpse of eternal splendor. Wow! Talk about out of this world.*
* *A body that may look old to others, but one that God sees as an instrument He can still use to accomplish His purposes.*
* *Young eyes that somehow know Jesus will give my old body the strength to accomplish more of His adventures.*

So all you aging bodies out there, comfort yourselves with this thought:

In Heaven's time I am considered a *Babe in the Woods*, and as far as eternity is concerned, my eyes and my body are both in the infancy stage.

JUST ENOUGH

"I have learned in whatever state I am, to be content." Philippians 4:11

God has given me just enough of everything to satisfy whatever need I have at the time. I don't need more of anything because He has given me just enough to be content.

God gave the Israelites just enough Manna for each day's need, just enough to fit the size of each family. When the Israelites tried to store more for a rainy day, they found the extra they had gathered turned rancid and filled with worms.

Isn't that the same for us today? When we are not satisfied with what we have, we become discontent. We begin to long for and gather more than we need. This does not bring us the contentment we thought it would, but actually turns rancid and sour in our spirit, and we begin to rot from within.

We slip away from our reliance on God to supply our needs to relying on our own selves. Thus our own selves are never satisfied with having just enough of God's provisions. That's when discontent becomes the norm in our lives.

Take me, for instance. God has given me enough hours in a day to accomplish whatever is needed for that day. The reason I believe I am short of hours is because I want to do more than what He has set aside. Thus I am always trying to cram in more, when He has given me just enough to accomplish what I can in a day. The choice is mine, and with it being obvious to God how much I can accomplish, why is it not obvious to me?

When I take a moment to look at what is on my list, when I compare it to what the day is throwing my way, when I pause and turn to Him for help, *"OK Lord, I'm over my head here. Please show me what is most important?"* When I do that, I immediately feel His peace about what I can leave undone.

In reality, the problem is my dissatisfaction in wanting to accomplish more when *just enough* is not *good enough* for me.

The secret to contentment is being satisfied with just enough of what God provides for us each day.

1912 – A VERY GOOD YEAR

"The days of our lives are seventy years; and if by reason of strength they are eighty years, Yet their boast is only labor and sorrow; For it is soon cut off, and we fly away." Psalm 90:10

Scripture tells us we have, on average, a lifespan of seventy or eighty years on this earth before we die. We know many people who don't even make the seventy years of toil and trouble before their life is over. But what about the few who go way past that timeline by twenty, thirty or more years?

We all know of someone who has not only accomplished this feat, but as society labels it they are *"very aware and with it."* They are living in the here and now, able to converse on many topics in a clear and logical manner. This is a wonderful blessing to family members who are helping with the care and well being of that elderly loved one.

The year of 1912 is dear to my heart because that is the year my mother was born. So in 2012 she turned 100, surpassing the seventy or eighty years allotted her. She has not, though, escaped the toil and sorrows nor the pains and problems that accompany an aging body.

When comparing my mother to many other elderly who are often much younger than her, the difference I find is in her attitude of gratitude. Her positive thinking and her strong faith in Jesus especially has carried her through the last year or so when she spent a few times in the hospital.

She spent months in a rehabilitation hospital learning to walk again after a broken hip. The doctors and nurses were amazed at how she responded to their care. All the while she made sure she kept them on their toes in regards to her recovery.

One often wonders why God takes some of us early while giving others a much longer time on earth. But one thing I do know that may give part answer to that question is that my mother was in her eighties before she became *Born Again*. Jesus knows our hearts and if or when we will accept or reject His offer of eternal life with Him.

Since my mother made that decision, she has been an avid reader of the Bible. Her faith has blossomed and strengthened her for this period of longevity in her life. She is and has been a beacon of light and encouragement to many friends she has made where she resides.

It has also been hard on her when she outlives the residents that have become close friends. Outliving her own family of eleven siblings, with her youngest sister dying in 2013 has been a difficult time, but she has remained cheerful and positive.

God has blessed my mother in so many ways. For the past twelve or so years God placed her at St. Hilda's in Toronto, which affords her a large measure of independence, and yet there is help readily available for any of her needs.

The majority of help has fallen on my sister Roberta who lives only twenty minutes away. She has often set aside her own plans in order to aid and comfort mom in ways that the rest of us siblings are unable to do because of distance or our own health problems.

I have come to believe totally in God's timing for anyone's life. All of us family members including her ten grandchildren and numerous great grandchildren look upon mom's longevity as a wonderful blessing. We have been given the opportunity to hear her life's story and glean much wisdom from the lessons she has learned the last one hundred years. Her positive attitude of gratitude for her life has been an inspiration to everyone who knows or meets her.

I gave my mother her first *Our Daily Bread*, which led to her mentioning she would like to have a Bible to look up passages that were listed. I then bought her one, which she had for some years before the print became too difficult for her to read. At that time my sister Maxine gave her a large print Bible. A while ago mom gave me back the Bible I had given her and in the front I found an amazing prayer she had written. From what I have observed of mom, God has fulfilled this prayer many times over. Following her prayer she wrote out Psalm 139:23-24. I asked her permission to share the prayer that she wrote so many years ago with my readers, and she graciously agreed.

Mom's Prayer —

"Almighty God, You know what I am undergoing. Help me to overcome. Don't let me become a pessimist. Preserve my optimistic outlook. I may lose many things, Father, but let me never lose my faith. Lord, You were the Undergoer who became the Overcomer. You died on the Cross; You Rose from the dead. Today hundreds of millions of people around the world know You, love You, respect You, admire You, draw inspiration and life from You. You promise to be my friend. You promise that if I keep believing, I will win. You Promise! Give me the courage to overcome the negative feelings that may depress my spirit, deflate my hopes and defuse my enthusiasm. My Faith tells me that I have Your Power within me now, because You are standing beside me, encouraging me all the way with Your promise... "Victory will be Yours, My Friend."

Thank You, Jesus Christ. Amen. Ella-May Olivero

Mom's favorite Scripture —

1912 – A Very Good Year

"Search me, O God, and know my heart; test me and know my anxious thoughts. See if there is any offensive way in me, and lead me in the way everlasting." Psalm 139:23-24

My mother at this moment still resides at St. Hilda's in her own apartment, making her own breakfast, but going down to the dining room for lunch and dinner. She has many caregivers who help her throughout the day, and she still has an optimistic outlook with a wonderful sense of humor. She still reads her Bible every day along with RBC's Our Daily Bread.

Hallelujah, what a Savior!

DEATH'S VICE

"I do not want you to be ignorant... concerning those who have fallen asleep, lest you sorrow as others who have no hope." 1 Thessalonians 4:13-18

Death. Such a final word. A word that brings fear to the heart and soul of man. Fear of the unknown. The passing of years of memories before ones eyes, or for some, a short burst in time. A time of tears, heartache, adjustment in daily lives. How one longs for the normal of what used to be....

Preparing for a future without your best friend, lover, and soul mate. Someone you laughed, cried, labored with, and encouraged when times were hard.

Coping with sudden feelings of helplessness that at times overwhelms you with anxiety. A grasping for moments to share before the inevitable happens.

Tears, tears and more tears bursting forth, falling desperately down your face, restricting the throat and heaving the chest with sobs. Grasping for more precious moments and memories together before there are no more tomorrows.

Run. Run. Escape... There must be another way. Another medicine. An herb, a vitamin, a treatment to extend the inevitable—to give more time.

Time? Right now there is some time. Preparation time for a funeral to come.

Right now, in this time, a cold vice-like void threatens to swallow you up into nothingness!

Then... *what is that seeping in through the gloom and despair... bursting forth in your mind... crumbling the finality of death . . . a song . . .*

Up from the grave He arose
With a mighty triumph o'er His foes.
He arose a victor from the dark domain;
And He lives forever with His Saints to reign...
He arose! He arose!
Hallelujah Christ arose!

The void becomes filled with hope, gladness, joy. Loving hands lifting, cradling, comforting, assuring.

Faithful hands that have overcome death because...
Up from the grave He did rise and He lives today!

He promises eternal life to those who believe in Him.
"I believe and my loved one believes."
He promises to carry not only me but also my loved one through this valley of death.
He promises a new body to replace our sick, decaying one.
He promises. He has proven to me, to the world, He is faithful and true.
He promises, "I trust and believe."

The anxiety is gone for now, and His love and peace comfort and enfold me.

I know Death's Vice will come again, but I also know He will be there to reach for my hand because ... *UP FROM THE GRAVE HE AROSE.*

WHEN HEAVEN IS MY HOME

When heaven is my home
And Christ is on His throne
There will be no more years,
death or tears
When heaven is my home.

When Christ comes back for me
From pain I'll be set free
No more ills, pills,
taxes or bills
When Christ comes back for me.

I will sing and shout
When I break free
From these earthly cares
That cling to me
When heaven is my home.

LIFEBLOOD

"An indispensable source of vitality or life."

Looking at a cover of a winter edition of *Our Daily Bread*, the lacy frost covering the tree branches in a field of sparkling snow, I wondered how the trees could ever again bring forth a landscape of green leaves or colorful perfumed blossoms. Then I remembered the lifeblood of the tree is buried deep in its roots, beyond the frozen ground, into soft fertile soil. Soil that is protecting it from the elements that would bring about its destruction.

Lifeblood. That word holds such a powerful meaning for me now. With it I am breathing, walking, thinking, feeling, going daily about life's activities. Without it, I'm cold, frozen, unthinking, unfeeling, immobile, hopeless, and dead.

There is a book about life that talks about another type of lifeblood. This book tells how this lifeblood melts the cold, dead body, bringing it into everlasting warmth and life. If you haven't read it, it is called the *Bible*, and the lifeblood mentioned in it is through God's son Jesus whose roots run deep into soft fertile soil.

Like the roots of the trees, Jesus *(if we allow Him)* is down deep in our souls protecting us from the cold elements above, protecting us from the paralyzing lies of the devil, who loves to tell us that life is hopeless, and we will be forever dead.

There comes a time in everyone's life when one seems to be frozen with grief and pain, numbly taking part in life's chores with a heart that seems shattered into a million pieces. A heart held together with the only glue that can adhere to the cold, Jesus. Jesus, who's warming, comforting arms, are slowly melting the pieces of my heart, and gluing it back together again. Forever changed, but healed.

Lifeblood. God's Word: the recipe for a heart that is temporarily or, like some, permanently frozen. The only recipe for a blossoming son-filled life here on earth, as well as in the hereafter.

Jesus, surrounding me with the prayers of loved ones. Lifting me into His comforting arms through the arms and hands of believers and unbelievers alike.

Jesus, who is slowly melting my frost ladened heart, and carrying me into the spring of a new beginning. I see His mercies, His **Lifeblood**, everywhere I go.

> *'Twas He who taught me thus to pray*
> *And I know He has answered prayer,*
> *But it has been in such a way*
> *As almost drove me to despair.*
> *Anon*

THE FIG TREE

My heart feels like it is in limbo
withered like the fig tree
never again to bear fruit.
Drained of life and
useless now...
Gnarled and dead.
Once filled with hope
now a meaningless void.
God, where are You?
Do you hear me
see me in this withered state
longing
to feel once again?
Only You
can bring back life
to this shriveled branch
change useless to meaningful.
Only You...
My God and my Savior.

Can the dead be brought back to life?
The withered to flourish
once again

*filling this void from
empty to full...
from bareness to fruitfulness?
Do not curse me to
the same fate as the fig tree.
Do not abandon me
but hear my cry
heal my broken spirit.
Fill this void
with Your presence
this withered branch
with Your life and renewal.
Bring purpose ...
A vision of hope and
encouragement
to this Saint in limbo.*

A SHEPHERD'S LOVE

"A Psalm of David . . . The Lord Is My Shepherd . . . Psalm 23"

'The Lord is my Shepherd' is a Psalm I memorized when I was a young girl. It is one Scripture that has stuck solidly in my memory, even through my dry years away from the Lord. I have called on it occasionally over the years to help me through difficult times, or just to fill me with peace. Sometimes I would recite it out loud, but most often say it quietly to myself. It never failed to bring me comfort.

For a couple of months after my husband's death, I would recite it two or three times a night before I would finally fall to sleep. It was then when I most needed God's promise of laying me down to rest in a green pasture beside a still water. My soul cried out in anguish to be comforted, held, soothed, and encouraged. I needed to be reminded every day and night of His love and care for me, that He really would never leave me.

It is now over six months since my husband died. He died at home with family beside him on December 31, 2010, at 11:38 p.m., just a little before midnight on New Year's Eve.

"The Lord is my Shepherd I shall not want. He maketh me to lie down in green pastures; he leadeth me beside the still waters."

Without the Lord as my Shepherd, I don't know how I would be in anything else but want. The Lord supplied all my wants or needs during this pain-filled time. He sent family members, relatives and friends to show me His love in so many tangible ways.

Each day I seemed to walk around totally relying on them to do whatever needed to be done whether this was preparing food for me to eat, washing my clothes, fixing broken household items, or helping me tend to all my legal affairs. Whatever my need was at the time, God supplied the person to do the job.

On the day of the funeral my daughter Karen had to help me dress and make the decision about what I should wear. Our roles reversed with me being the little girl needing help, and she being the mother lovingly tending to my need, all the while dealing with her own breaking heart at the loss of her father.

"He restoreth my soul."

I trusted what His Word told me, and He continued to restore my strength, my faith, the healing of my body, while restoring peace to my soul.

"He leadeth me in paths of righteousness for His names sake."

At night when I could not pray, my two daughters-in-law, Donna and Grace, came to my bedside, and as we held hands they prayed the words I could not say. They did this every night for the whole month they were with me. Finally the last night before they left for home, God enabled me to pray.

"Yea though I walk through the valley of the shadow of death, I will fear no evil."

His protection for me from the *evil one* was unnoticed by me during this time as I never felt any evil near me. I felt only His love through those He placed around me.

While I walked through the valley of my husband's death, I knew that my loved one was in heaven not hell. Having this knowledge brought unbelievable comfort to my aching heart because I too trust in Jesus that we will be united again someday. Jesus is our Savior, our Shepherd who has claimed us for His own.

"...for Thou art with me, Thy rod and Thy staff they comfort me. Thou preparest a table before me in the presence of mine enemies: Thou anointest my head with oil; my cup runneth over."

"How are you doing?" people continue to ask me with genuine interest and caring. I don't hesitate to tell them I am doing well. Not that I don't miss my husband of almost fifty-five years. I miss his laughter, his wonderful sense of humor, his unique love of adventure....

Like the time we were driving on an old country road he traversed as a young man. He never blinked an eye, as the road got narrower, and narrower, until it was two ruts running through a farmer's field before—back into the bush we went. I worried along the way about being yelled at, shot at, or what if we couldn't find a place to turn the car around? But none of that ever happened. What fun we had, and what joy those memories are for me now.

How I miss his adventurous spirit. I have to force myself to step outside my comfort zone. I needed him to grab my hand and pull me along. He never seemed to mind though and would laugh and encourage me along the way. He never referred to me as being a drag or holding him back from his adventures.

I miss his wonderful mind; his fantastic ability to remember facts; he was so knowledgeable on so many subjects, that I still momentarily think, *"I'll ask Neil,"* before I remember I can't do that anymore.

He was an excellent teacher and administrator who always put children's concerns first and foremost, a loving father, faithful husband, talented musician ... just an all-round perfect kind of guy. Ain't love grand?

My cup runneth over for almost fifty-five years, and I have no indication that God will not continue to bless me, as this wonderful Psalm ends,

"Surely goodness and mercy shall follow me all the days of my life: and I will dwell in the house of the Lord forever."

Forever with Jesus? What a wonderful legacy of hope.

As you can see memories, are coming easier for me now, and in between them I keep myself busy with whatever the Lord puts before me. My family, church family, relatives and friends, are still being sent to love, care, help and encourage me daily. What more could one ask of a Shepherd's love?

If our greatest need had been information, God would have sent an educator.
If our greatest need had been technology, God would have sent us a scientist.
If our greatest need had been money, God would have sent us an economist.
But since our greatest need was forgiveness, God sent us a Savior.
Anon

I HAD A DREAM

"If you could glimpse heaven for just one minute – or even one second – you would never say again that this life is better."
Billy Graham

The Bible tells us that God has spoken to many people through dreams and that they understood what the dreams meant.

Take Mary's husband Joseph, for example. God spoke four times to him through dreams in reference to what actions he should take. The first dream told him to take Mary as his wife even though he knew she was pregnant, but not by him. The second dream told him to flee from Bethlehem to Egypt with Mary and Jesus when Herod schemed to kill all children in Bethlehem two years of age and under. The third dream told Joseph to leave Egypt and go back to

Israel. And the fourth dream told him to return to live in the town of Nazareth.

Dream is the name of a beautiful song that my two granddaughters, Sara and Amanda, sang at Neil's funeral. It tells about flying away to the highest heights, finally being free from these earthly bonds. I have often wondered what it would be like to get a glimpse of the afterlife as some on earth have experienced.

The night Neil died, our son Robert was blessed with a glimpse of this when he heard the most beautiful music and wonderful *Jam Session* going on with Neil playing a guitar and singing. The joy he felt was wonderful and comforting to him at a time he was so low in grief. He looked around wondering where the music was coming from before he realized it was God's gift to him, showing him his father was well and happy. I envied him that experience, wishing it could have been me. However, God chooses how, when, and to whom He speaks, and he gives what is needed most for that person at the time.

Well, God spoke to me one year later, early in the morning when I had a dream. Let me tell you about it.

Neil and I were driving in our old blue Ram Charger looking for a parts and repair place we needed for the Ram. We drove too far, and for some reason we missed the place. The next thing I knew, we were in a man's house that was three stories high. I was sitting by myself on a lounge chair in the living room on the second floor, trying to finish eating slices of ham that had been rolled up in one large roll. I could not finish it as each time I bit into it, it seemed to stay the same size. It had no flavor nor did I enjoy eating it, but I would not throw it away.

Off the living room were sliding glass doors with a balcony outside and stairs at the side leading to the patio and entrance below. There were couples everywhere on the balcony as well as below chatting and talking while music was playing. I neither heard what anyone was saying, nor the kind of music being played. I just knew it was.

While I was alone in the living room, the man that owned the house came up to me and told me we had missed the parts place, which was back down the street at 1931. He told me to leave right away before they closed and seemed in a hurry to get us there.

I ran out to the balcony holding this ham roll and called twice for Neil. Someone told me he was below so I went to the balcony edge and looking down, called once again for Neil.

He came out from a corner behind some people and shuffled forward, very puffy in baggy pants with his waist and legs large and swollen. He could not hear me as I tried to tell him about the repair shop. He stepped up to a small landing and indicated with his hands that he could not hear me, but he never tried to speak.

Neil seemed to be in the crowd, but apart from it, and not partaking of the conversations around him. Yet the people knew he was there since they told him I was calling. He seemed irritated that I had called him out from where he had been.

As he stood there, his bulky pants fell down to his knees revealing his underpants and emphasizing his bloated legs and upper body. He reached to get them, but they dropped farther to his feet. As he reached down farther and was pulling them back up, I noticed he was no longer bloated but was a normal size again.

There continued to be a lot of talking and music going on around us, so I signaled to him and shouted that I would come downstairs through the inside of the house. I went inside and up to the third floor to get our things together. All the while I was trying to finish eating this rolled up meat that never seemed to get any smaller.

At this point, I woke up and immediately knew the meaning of the dream. It is as vivid to me today as it was that morning.

Our old Ram Charger was Neil's body needing a new part, which was his heart. The man I didn't know who owned the house was an angel sent to comfort me as the first anniversary of Neil's death approached.

The many slices of rolled up ham was telling me that the problem was bigger than I could handle, but at the same time I wouldn't stop trying to get a handle on it.

The three-story house was the three heart attacks Neil had suffered over the years.

The people everywhere talking with music playing was life going on around us normally that we were oblivious to as we struggled to overcome each hurdle.

The balcony edge was where I stood and watched Neil's life and death struggle, so many times over the years.

The parts place down the street at 1931 is the year that Neil was born. The parts and repair place was Heaven, where Neil would receive this needed new part. The man *(angel)* was in a hurry for us to leave the house because Neil's earthly time was running out.

Me alone in the living room. Many times I was alone telling God I wasn't ready to let Neil go. He had mercy and kept the roll whole until I could not bite into it anymore.

Neil coming out from behind people and shuffling over to the stairway. God gave me another glimpse of what life was like for Neil his last years. The pants falling down clearly brought back memories of what state his body was in here on earth, and as he pulled the pants back up it revealed the freedom from that discomfort and pain that he is now experiencing in heaven.

I understand why Neil was displeased at being brought out. Would you be happy to leave heaven and come back to earth to an old body that caused you so much grief and pain?

I thanked God for giving me another glimpse of Neil's last year. I also thanked Him for the comfort He had provided me through this dream. It reminded me once again, to keep my eyes focused on Him, for the gift He has given Neil, He will also give to me.

God speaks to each of us every day in a very special way through the gift of His son Jesus. Many Prophets had dreams or visions that told of the Messiah to come. We, on the other hand, have the privilege to know He has come and to know Him personally.

May you partake of this wonderful gift given us by a merciful and loving Father.

A BRIGHTER NEW YEAR

From sinking sand He lifted me,
With tender hand He lifted me,
From shades of night to plains of light,
O praise His name, He lifted me! Gabriel

As I have previously related, January 2011 was, for me, the beginning of a sorrowful year. I had lost my husband the night before on New Year's Eve 2010. I felt a great gap in me — like my right arm was missing, but at any moment it would suddenly reappear and reattach itself. I waited and waited, all the while thinking that soon all would be normal again. But it never happened. A new normal was born to me that night in 2010.

I don't remember much at all of 2011. I was very sick through the first few months with flu and nosebleeds. The nosebleeds ended the night my daughter Karen and I went on a harrowing ride through a snowstorm, me by ambulance, while Karen followed behind in her car to the hospital in Barrie over an hour away. Total exhaustion seemed to permeate my very being that year.

I do remember my family lovingly tending to my needs, from the health problems mentioned above to helping me grasp all the legal paperwork required. They were right beside me during the huge learning curve that taking total ownership requires. The extra load of running a household previously shared by two pairs of shoulders still occasionally rears its unwanted head.

I was on an airplane a couple of times that year to visit my sons Tim and Garth in California. I also took a few road trips to visit relatives, but don't ask me what they were about because all I recall are snippets here and there.

My memory began to reappear by the end of 2011 when I spent a very pleasant Christmas with my daughter Karen before going to my son Robert's for five enjoyable days. From Robert's home in Toronto, I took another flight to California to spend New Years 2012 with my sons Tim and Garth and their families.

We shared a good New Year's celebration with some shed tears, but also much laughter as we told stories of a much loved husband, father and grandfather. We were filled with peace as we remembered the strong faith we all shared, knowing it would be a wonderful reunion when we met him again one day in heaven.

In the past I dealt with life's disappointments through physical work. If you found me scrubbing floors or washing walls, it was a strong indication I was in some form of forced therapy.

God however, had other plans this time around with the return of my energy. I became more aware of others who were dealing with their own difficult problems and needing a helping hand.

I found myself supplying respite to a sister from her caregiving burdens to my mother: I helped another sister to recover from a shoulder operation, I spent time helping my mother in her recovery from a broken hip, plus many other opportunities that God put before me. Helping others in their healing process shifted the focus off myself, and I became a blessing while being blessed.

Now 2012 was ending on a different upbeat note with me opting to have Christmas and New Years here in the comfort of my own home. A brighter vision for 2013 began by filling me with a joyful and positive attitude.

To add to this feeling of well being, my grandson Joshua came to live with me while he worked in the area salting away his earnings to help further his education. It was a fun, learning time for a granny in her seventies, and a twenty one year old. Patience was needed on both sides as we tried to decipher what we were actually trying to communicate to one another. However, I believe you can teach an old dog new tricks, and young dogs have a lot they can learn from an old dog.

Recently, I was reading Neil's favorite Scripture, Psalm 121. This time around I had a better insight as to why it was so special to him. See for yourself what he took to heart. He loved the poetry of the King James version below.

"I will lift up mine eyes unto the hills, from whence cometh my help.
My help cometh from the Lord, which made heaven and earth.
He will not suffer thy foot to be moved: He that keepeth thee will not slumber.

*Behold, he that keepeth Israel shall neither slumber nor sleep.
The LORD is thy keeper: the LORD is thy shade upon thy right hand.
The sun shall not smite thee by day, nor the moon by night.
The LORD shall preserve thee from all evil: he shall preserve thy soul.
The LORD shall preserve thy going out and thy coming in from this time forth, and even for evermore." Psalm 121*

THE DIFFICULT JOB OF A GUARDIAN ANGEL

He will fill your mouth with laughter and your lips with shouts of joy. Job 8:21

I think my Guardian Angel has been falling down on the job. I say this in all sincerity and I will tell you why. I have become much too serious about this life I'm living on earth's planet. I used to have a sense of humor, but it has been stolen by someone or something. Where was my Guardian Angel when that happened?

I don't look in mirrors much anymore because every time I do, this old lady looks back at me. I don't know what or how, but I figure it must be some sort of magic trick because I haven't seen myself in years. My Guardian Angel must know the answer, but why hasn't he told me?

Another thing. When I get together with friends they ask me *"What have you been up to lately?"* Now I know I have been going straight out doing many things, but do you think I can remember any of it? Noooo. What comes out of my mouth is some lame thing like, *"I had a poached egg for breakfast."* Or some other such nonsense. I need my Guardian Angel to get back on the job by locating and retrieving my memory.

I must say, though, that my Guardian Angel did redeem himself somewhat lately. I invited my friend Lillian over to watch a movie, since I had not seen my sense of humor for some time. Lillian always brings a chuckle or two right along with her.

So after I put a movie into the machine, we settled down munching on some fruit, crackers and cheese, looking forward to being entertained. I had not seen this movie before and it turned out to be a serious, not very memorable, but okay type of movie that I doubt I'll ever watch again. I'm sure Lillian felt the same way because by the time it ended she was ready for a nap.

So I began to search my collection for something that might be a little more entertaining and came upon an old movie I've watched many times over the years, which always brings me a laugh, or two. I mentioned this to Lillian who was agreeable to give me another chance, so into the machine it went.

Well, we were not long into the movie before we began to laugh. Not just a chuckle or two, but deep down belly laughs. You know, the kind where tears roll down your face while you hold onto your aching stomach trying to take in the next breath.

This went on through most of the movie and when it was over we felt so happy, full of the joy of life with thanks to God for laughter, along with the blessing of friendship.

Lillian gathered her things together and went off home with the movie in her hands, thinking it was something her daughter and two grandchildren would enjoy during the winter break. However, the *best laid plans*, as the old saying goes, makes that another story I'll let Lillian tell.

What was the name of the movie that brought us such gales of laughter? Why it was that old goody, *"The gods must be crazy."*

Thank you Guardian Angel. I'm so glad to see your back on the job. Now, tell me, is there anything you can do to get rid of that old lady in my mirror? What, you need more time you say?

LANTERN & ANCHOR

"We have this hope as an anchor for the soul, firm and secure. It entered the inner sanctuary behind the curtain, where our forerunner, Jesus, has entered on our behalf. He has become a high priest forever, in the order of Melchizedek." Hebrews 6:19-20

The old saying goes, *"It's always darkest before the storm."* That may be true, but the storm tosses you back and forth, crashing you into the unknown while you frantically try to get your feet back on solid ground.

The darkness brings with it the fear of the unknown, the storm the anguish of the known.

In the storm you try to grab hold of anything solid to keep you from being flung about like a rag doll. The darkness keeps you trying to grasp the mist.

You know it's there when you grab for it; then it evaporates before your very eyes, slipping away untouched.

How does one survive the darkness that creeps into one's life unwanted and unbidden?

What does one do when the storms of life threaten to send you crashing into unwanted territory?

The answer is obvious. You need to have a Lantern to light your way when the darkness descends, and an Anchor to keep you weighted to one spot so you won't be tossed to and fro in the fray.

Years ago I found my lantern, *"The Light of the world,"* and my anchor, *"upon this Rock I will build my church,"* in Jesus Christ. As long as I kept my eyes focused on Him, then my path was lit up brightly so I could see the way clearly.

His love continues to light my way through some very dark oppressive tunnels, always bringing me safely through to the other side.

Through all the storms that have raged around me trying to knock me off my feet, His Word has always anchored me to that solid rock. He never lets go of my hand, and He never will because He has told me. *"Never will I leave you, never will I forsake you."*

Are you groping in the darkness? Do you feel like you're being tossed about like a rag doll?

Jesus is waiting for you with His lantern and His anchor, and if you let Him, I guarantee you will never be afraid of the dark or be tossed about by the storms of life again.

Part of a poem written by Marie Louise Haskins –

I said to the man who stood at the Gate of the Year,
'Give me a light that I may tread safely
into the unknown.' And he replied,
'Go out into the darkness, and put your hand
into the Hand of God. That shall be to you better
than light, and safer than a known way.'

DISAPPOINTMENT– HIS APPOINTMENT

"You have turned for me my mourning into dancing." Psalm 30:11

There are many things that bring disappointment into our lives. We can be disappointed with our political leaders; our children; our relatives; our friends; our parents; our church, our pastor; ourselves; with God.

We are disappointed when we are taken for granted, when others don't see our problems, when special moments in our lives are ignored or forgotten. Or when we feel that others have forgotten us completely.

Forgotten? Perhaps. But whatever the reason for your disappointment there is only one way to deal with it and that is to arrange an appointment with

God through prayer. Tell Him how you are hurting and why you are disappointed. Wrestle with Him as Jacob wrestled to get the answer he needed.

Can't see it yet? Then keep wrestling and bringing it before Him until your 'why' questions are replaced by a trust in God to supply the answers needed at that time.

Somewhere along the line you will work it out with Him, and your attitude will change direction. If you do not forgive whomever you feel is disappointing you, you will carry that disappointment forward for another and another and another day, until the weight of it becomes unbearable.

Soon you will notice your name has changed from Naomi (pleasant) to Mara (bitter). Bitterness will only lead you into more disappointment, not only towards others but also with yourself. After all, how many people have you disappointed in the past without being aware of doing so?

We all face disappointment throughout our lives, but be encouraged. The pain of disappointment can be soothed with a heart of gratitude.

Randy Kilgore writes,

"When Jesus promised He would never leave us alone, He meant in the hard times as well as in the good times ... Look for God in your difficult place and discover what He's doing in and through you there" (Our Daily Bread – September 20/13).

Listen carefully *(that is not an easy thing to do)*, and wait *(even harder still)* for His direction. Then act upon those directions, and make the necessary adjustments to your life.

Turn your life from disappointment to an appointment to meet with God who will help lift you up and over your disappointments.

ANXIOUS PRAYERS

Helen Steiner Rice
A Collection of Encouragement

When we are deeply disturbed by a problem
and our minds are filled with doubt,
And we struggle to find a solution,
but there seems to be no way out,
We futilely keep on trying
to untangle our web of distress,
But our own little, puny efforts
meet with very little success.
And finally, exhausted and weary,
discouraged and downcast and low,
With no foreseeable answer
which we fully expect right away . . . .
But God can't get through to the anxious,
who are much too impatient to wait,
You have to believe in God's promise
that He comes not too soon or too late . . . .
So be not impatient or hasty,
just trust in the Lord and believe,
For whatever you ask in faith and love,
in abundance you are sure to receive.

FAITH LIKE SOLOMON OR JABEZ

"Meaningless! Meaningless!" says the Teacher. "Utterly meaningless! Everything is meaningless." Ecclesiastes1:1

As one ages, the momentum in one's life slows down, with a tendency to look back more often than perhaps one should. Remembering what once was with fondness comes easily, but always following close behind are the memories of roads taken that led to sorrow and regret. The ambitions that at one time seemed so paramount to make my life feel important are no longer a priority that defines my success. My ambitions are now completely focused elsewhere. Solomon accomplished more in his short life than most of us even dream about, and he was only in his sixties when he died. Before Solomon departed this world, he looked upon his past life and dubbed it, *"meaningless."*

Now, Solomon started out well, but somewhere along the way he took his focus off what was meaningful, the One and Only true God, and put it onto meaningless other gods. He lived his life for the world's pleasures and came up with an empty soul. I know how Solomon felt because I was once there myself.

I have a tendency to look back, more so since my husband died, or perhaps it's an age-related thing. I love to remember the good times instead of the struggles and hard lessons I had to learn, which keep popping unbidden into the forefront of my mind, the lessons that molded me into the person I am today. The person I would not be if I had not learned from those lessons. Looking back can be a good thing if one remembers that the reason the good times are so good is because the bad times uncover them.

I fully believe God directs our path in life, unless of course one continues to renounce His very existence. When that happens, He will leave us to our own devices.

It is very different, though, when at some point in your life you have accepted Jesus as your Savior. Then, if you keep pushing Him away with *"I'll call you when I need you,"* He will oblige by giving you that extra length of rope. However, just before you hang yourself with it, He will reign you in with these very lessons you would like to forget. Think of it as putting iron in the fire to temper it into strong steel.

These lessons that I regret and want to forget have tempered me and made me into a stronger person with a strong faith. I would not be this way if I had not learned from those lessons.

When you look back, don't get caught up in the depressing thoughts of what might have been. God can use your past failures to help others who are at those same crossroads you once traversed.

So what do you do when you find your life meaningless like Solomon? You do what Jabez did, and you change your momentum by changing your circumstances.

Jabez is not remembered for what he did but for what he prayed. It is a short little paragraph or two in 1 Chronicles 4:9-10 that tells us his mother called him Jabez because she *"bore him in pain."* How would you like to go around with a name that means you caused someone much pain?

This passage also tells us that Jabez was more honorable than his brothers and that he loved God. He was not content to go through life thinking he was meaningless. He had faith that God could and would change his circumstances. The key here is Jabez had *faith*.

You are never too old to change your circumstances and acquire the same faith as Jabez. Instead of wallowing in memories of your past sins, be amazed at how God can use your past in miraculous ways today. You can do this by praying the same prayer daily that Jabez prayed.

I began to pray this prayer a while ago, and I can tell you from experience that this very prayer has brought me amazing blessings. I am able to do things for which I have no skills or training, and barriers once closed to me have come tumbling down.

So, like Jabez, change your momentum, and begin to ask God to bless you as He blessed Jabez.

And what is Jabez's prayer?

"Jabez cried out to the God of Israel,
'Oh that you would bless me indeed,
and enlarge my territory,
that Your hand would be with me,
And that You would keep me from evil.
That I may not cause pain.'
So God granted him what he requested."
1 Chronicles 4:10 NKJ

FURTHER ENCOURAGEMENT

As I have gathered these articles together for this book, I am filled with awe and thanksgiving towards what my Savior has done in my life. I would be so destitute without Him that I shudder at that prospect.

If you don't know Jesus, I pray this book will have encouraged you to seek Him out. I guarantee, if you do this, your life will never again be the same.

CPSIA information can be obtained at www.ICGtesting.com
Printed in the USA
LVOW08s2050300914

406606LV00004B/13/P